GREAT BIBLE QUESTIONS

Dr. Derek Stringer

Copyright Good News Broadcasting Association (UK)

Good News Broadcasting Association (UK)
Ranskill DN22 8NN England
Email: info@gnba.net Web site: www.gnba.net

Scripture taken from the
HOLY BIBLE
NEW INTERNATIONAL VERSIONS
Copyright 1973, 1978, 1984
International Bible Society.
Used by permission of Zondervan.
All rights reserved.

No parts of this publication may be reproduced, stored in a retrieval system, or transmitted in any form or by any means, electronic, mechanical, photocopying, recording or otherwise without the prior permission of the copyright owner.

British Library Cataloguing In Publication Data
A Record of this Publication is available
from the British Library

ISBN 978-1-84685-959-5

First Published 2008 by
Exposure Publishing,
an imprint of
Diggory Press Ltd
Three Rivers, Minions, Liskeard, Cornwall, PL14 5LE, UK
WWW.DIGGORYPRESS.COM

ACKNOWLEDGEMENTS

My grateful thanks to David and Pat Holme for their skills in proof-reading. Any mistakes that you find in this book I am responsible for, not them. My thanks also go to my colleague here at GNBA Chalmers Dobson for checking the content and as far as possible the sources of material.

I like what Brian Mavis has written in sermoncentral.com:

"Even people who think that they are being completely original are probably not quite right. Some copy ideas without even knowing it. Rick Warren (a very copied preacher) is known for saying, "If you take an idea from one person it is called plagiarism. If you take ideas from a number of people it is called research." Ironically, even that was said before, by US playwright Wilson Mizner (1876-1933). He said, "Copy from one, it's plagiarism; copy from two, it's research." John F. Kennedy is credited for saying, "Ask not what your country can do for you—ask what you can do for your country." But it was really his ghost-writer, John Kenneth Galbraith, who wrote it. And Galbraith may have lifted the idea from Oliver Wendell Holmes who said, "We... recall what our country has done for each of us, and to ask ourselves what we can do for our country in return."

In my *research* for this book I have gone to several sources including SermonCentral where pastors share material with one another. Some of the ideas, quotes and illustrations in these chapters came from Pastor David Dykes in Texas and Pastor Mark Adams of Redlands Baptist Church Virginia. God bless you in your ministries.

DEDICATION

This book is lovingly dedicated to my wife, Pauline, daughters Tracy and Clare, not forgetting my son-in-law Tony. Thank you for being the constant encouragement that you are to me in the ministry the Lord has entrusted.

Contents

		Page
Chapter 1	Am I My Brother's Keeper?	
	Genesis 4:1-9	7
Chapter 2	Where Is The Lamb?	
	Genesis 22:1-19	23
Chapter 3	Who Have I in Heaven but You?	
	Psalm 73	41
Chapter 4	Can Guests Fast?	
	Luke 5:33-39	58
Chapter 5	What are you Doing Here?	
	Kings 19	79
Chapter 6	How Many Times Shall I Forgive?	
	Matthew 18:21	93
Chapter 7	Has God Forgotten to be Merciful?	
	Psalm 77	108
Chapter 8	Do Not Touch?	
	Colossians 2:13-23	129
Chapter 9	Who Can Stand...?	
	1Samuel 17:1-51	152
Chapter 10	What is that in Your Hand?	
	Exodus 3 & 4	166
Chapter 11	Where Are You?	
	Genesis 3:1-21	181
Chapter 12	Do You Love Me?	
	John 21: 1-9	201
Chapter 13	How Can I Be Sure of This?	
	Luke 1:5-25	219
Chapter 14	Why Have You Forsaken Me?	
	Psalm 22	237
Chapter 15	How have you loved us?	
	Malachi 1:1-14	253
Chapter 16	Who Is Worthy?	
	Revelation 5	272

Introduction

A student in a philosophy class was taking his first examination. On the paper there was a single line that simply said: *"Is this a question? - Discuss."*

After a short time he wrote: *"If that is a question, then this is an answer."* The student received an "A" in the class.

Philosophy. We sometimes think of it as a subject where everyone sits around in a class asking ridiculous questions ("If a tree falls in the forest and no one is around to hear it . . ."). But the word "philosophy" comes from a Greek word meaning "love of wisdom" and that is something the Bible speaks positively about:

"Blessed is the man who finds wisdom, the man who gains understanding." Proverbs 3:13.

It is important to understand what the Bible means by "wisdom". The best definition I know is this: *"The ability to make right decisions"*.

To do that we must listen to God. The Bible says:

"The fear of the LORD is the beginning of knowledge, but fools despise wisdom and discipline." Proverbs 1:7.

May God bless you in your pursuit of wisdom! My prayer is that by studying some key Biblical questions we will not spend time but invest it in ways that outlast it.

Derek Stringer

Good News Broadcasting Association (UK)
Ranskill DN22 8NN England

Chapter 1   Genesis 4:1-9

Am I My Brother's Keeper?

Children are full of questions. If you are a parent you know what we are talking about. In this questioning stage our children's non-stop inquiries can be tiring as they ask, "why this?" "why that?" "what is this?" "what is that?" "where are we going?" "when will we get there?" and so on. We know that parents should be patient during this stage because children need to ask questions. If they do not ask, they will never learn. They will never get the answers they require in order to grow up and mature.

This does remind me of the little boy who asked his dad how far away the Earth was from the Sun. His dad said, "I do not know son." "Well how far away is the Earth from Mars?" I do not know son." "Well dad, how far away is the Earth from Pluto?" "I do not know son." The boy said, "Dad, you don't mind me asking you these questions do you?" He said, "No son, of course not. I mean, if you never ask you will never learn." Exactly!

I mention this because the fact is that adults need to ask questions as well as children and get answers! Seeking answers for the questions of life is an important part of the spiritual growth and maturity of a Christian. I think Jesus implied this in His Sermon on the Mount when He said:

> "...everyone who asks receives; and he who seeks, finds..."
> Luke 11:10.

In this book we do some asking and seeking together by studying the answers to some of the great questions of the

Bible. Here are answers that we need in order to find and receive the understanding that we require to grow and mature as God's children. I do not know about you but I am very excited about this study. There are a lot of things that I both need and want to learn from the texts surrounding all these truly great questions.

Our first question is the first recorded question ever asked by a human being: The question Cain asked God:

"Am I my brother's keeper?" Genesis 4:9.

Let us look at the text surrounding it in Genesis Chapter 4:

Adam lay with his wife Eve, and she became pregnant and gave birth to Cain. She said, "With the help of the LORD I have brought forth a man." Later she gave birth to his brother Abel. Now Abel kept flocks, and Cain worked the soil. In the course of time Cain brought some of the fruits of the soil as an offering to the LORD. But Abel brought fat portions from some of the firstborn of his flock. The LORD looked with favour on Abel and his offering, but on Cain and his offering he did not look with favour. So Cain was very angry, and his face was downcast. Then the LORD said to Cain, "Why are you angry? Why is your face downcast? If you do what is right, will you not be accepted? But if you do not do what is right, sin is crouching at your door; it desires to have you, but you must master it." Now Cain said to his brother Abel, "Let us go out to the field." And while they were in the field, Cain attacked his brother Abel and killed him. Then the LORD said to Cain, "Where is your brother Abel?" "I do not know," he replied. "Am I my brother's keeper?"

In order to glean all the information possible from this question and its answer, we need to go back and take a close look at all that has happened previously. Our text picks up right after Adam and Eve were banished from the Garden of Eden. Shortly after that, Eve became pregnant and gave birth to their first child.

Most parents have pride in their newborn children. They hope that their child will have a long and productive life. I know a few expectant parents are hoping this for their soon to be born children. However, to fully understand what happened here, we must grasp the fact that no parents in all of history have had more hope for a child than Adam and Eve had at the birth of Cain. Let me explain.

Adam and Eve had just been expelled from the Garden of Eden, their paradise on Earth. But before God told them they had to leave that wonderful place, He promised them a Deliverer. Genesis 3:15 tells us that after man sinned God told Satan *that this Deliverer, who would come from the "seed of a woman", would crush his head, destroying him and his works.*

Adam and Eve had never seen a child before. So, when it became obvious that a child was growing in Eve's womb, I believe they began to hope that this child would or could be the promised Deliverer, the One Who would crush the wicked, deceptive Satan and enable them to return to the Garden of Eden. They must have counted the months and days until finally the baby was born!

One reason I think they looked at their child in this way was because of the name they gave him. They called him "Cain," based on the Hebrew word, which means, "acquired." But in the context of their longing for the Deliverer to come, I think it is best translated: *"I have got him!"* or *"Here he is!"* Another thing that leads me to this conclusion is the literal translation of Genesis 4: 1. And to get to that literal translation we have to realise that in the Hebrew, the words, "with the help of" which we find in verse 1, are not there in the original Hebrew text. The NIV includes them because it is the way many translators think it should read. However, the most literal wording of Eve's statement in verse 1 would go like this *"I have brought forth a man, even the Lord!"*

Eve would not have been claiming to give birth to God. No, she just used the word for "the Lord" in the broader sense saying she brought forth "the one who gives life." By putting all this together I believe the best translation for Eve's statement would probably be this *"I have brought forth a man, even the Deliverer."*

In Adam and Eve's minds the life-giver had been born, the promised One who would destroy the evil work of Satan and give them back the life they wanted most, life in the Garden of Eden, Paradise! We can all understand how Adam and Eve felt. They remembered how wonderful life in the Garden was and they longed to return to it. We have no such memory to draw on but inside I think we still have the same yearning our very first ancestors had. We all long for Paradise. I do not know about you but the older I get the more I ache to be free of this evil world and be in Heaven with my Lord and all those who have been saved because He destroyed Satan's power when He died for our sins on the Cross. The more funeral services of loved ones and friends that I conduct and attend, the more I want all this aching to be over and to be in the place where there is no more pain, sorrow, or striving and no more suffering and death. A place where face-to-face I will see my Lord. It makes me impatient. I want to say *"Hurry up Jesus! Come back today! I am ready!"* I for one understand Adam and Eve's impatience for God's promised Deliverer!

In due time a second son was born to the world's first parents and he was named, "Abel" which means, "frail" suggesting that the physical effects of sin were already becoming apparent in the human race. Before the fall of man, that is, before Adam and Eve's sin, everything was perfect. But since then everything has been subject to:

"...bondage to decay." Romans 8:21.

Since sin entered the world, because it did, there has been sickness, ageing and death. Abel's name suggests that he was frail and sickly which is probably why, as verse 2 says, Cain, the stronger son, became a farmer doing backbreaking agricultural labour whereas Abel, the weaker son, became a shepherd, quietly tending the flocks.

Another thing we should note is this. The names of these first two children allude to the fact that there was a difference in the way their parents looked at them. Cain was the strong one, he was the favoured one, the one that they mistakenly thought of as "the promised deliverer", the "Here he is!" child. Abel was the weak one, he was the "frail...other child." It would be very easy for them to justify their favour of Cain, if they believed he was indeed a child of destiny, born to fulfil the great promise of God.

This brings a question to my mind. Could Adam and Eve's longing for the Deliverer, their belief that Cain was indeed the promised one and their favouritism have led them to spoil their first born? Could their perception have led them to plant the seeds of arrogance and conceit in Cain's heart? That is the question to keep in mind. Parents, as you read this, ask yourselves if you are teaching your children the importance of humility. Would it be more accurate to say that you are raising little "Cains" at home?

Verse 3 says that a time came when both brothers, now fully grown, came to present an offering to the Lord. This suggests that God must have given specific instruction about sacrifices to Adam and Eve and their descendants. For example, the words in verse 3 literally say *"at the end of days"* meaning that God had appointed a particular time period at the end of which sacrifices were to be offered. Perhaps this was done on a regular basis, once a season, or once a year.

I also think that there was a special place appointed for this act of worship. In the closing words of Chapter 3 God set the winged cherubim and a flaming sword at the gateway to Eden. Many centuries later, God told Moses how to make the Tabernacle, the Tent used for worship by the Children of Israel. God instructed him to make a mercy seat with cherubim whose wings would meet over this seat and offerings were to be placed on it. The Day of Atonement was consummated here. Once a year, the High Priest brought in a food offering on the Day of Atonement to sacrifice for the sins of all the people. It makes sense to conclude that this practice, described for us in Exodus, originated in Genesis here at the entrance to the Garden of Eden where the winged Cherubim stood. It is very likely that the gateway of Eden was itself the first mercy seat, where once a year Adam and Eve and their children were to come with an offering for the Lord. We do not know this for sure but it seems to make sense.

Verse 3 says that at one of these appointed times Cain brought some of the fruits of the soil, the fruit and produce he had harvested, to this first mercy seat as an offering for God. But as verse 4 says, Abel brought: *"fat portions from some of the firstborn of his flock."*

The Bible says the Lord looked on Abel's offering with favour, He accepted it but He rejected Cain's offering. At this point another question comes to mind, "How did these brothers know Cain's offering was rejected and Abel's accepted?" Genesis does not tell us but we get a clue from reading the Biblical accounts of Gideon and Elijah. When these men made offerings to God, fire came down from Heaven and consumed their offerings. It was an indication of God's acceptance of their sacrifices. So that is probably what happened here. Fire consumed Abel's offering but did not even touch Cain's offering.

I feel like a little child at this point, because this brings another question, a very important one, to my mind and perhaps yours: why did God accept Abel's offering but reject that of his elder brother? The Bible does not tell us so we can only look at the verses to see if there are clues that would indicate the reasons, so that we can learn how we should bring our offerings to God. There are at least three possibilities for us to consider.

- Their different attitudes towards the offerings.
- The different qualities of their offerings.
- What they chose to offer.

First: their ATTITUDES

Cain must have known that, as Genesis 3:17 tells us, *God had cursed the ground because of Adam and Eve's sin.* To give God an offering from the ground He had cursed would have been an insult to Him. It would be like serving dinner to a guest on dirty dishes. So, it is obvious that Cain's offering reflected a lack of reverence for God. But Cain's offering also reflected his conceit, his belief that due to his hard and careful work, done in his own strength, he had produced something from the cursed ground.

Maybe God rejected Cain's gift because he was too pleased

with himself. Perhaps his offering was given in pride. We know from the Letter of James that:

"God opposes the proud." James 4:6.

Whenever we give to God we do so as a symbol, a reminder of the fact that we would be nothing and have nothing if it was not for God's grace. Our offerings should be given in humility as a reverent act of worship.

Second: the QUALITY of their offerings

Abel brought "the first-lings of this flock and of the fat thereof." Genesis 4:4.

At that time, fat was considered to be the choicest part of an animal. So, in other words, this text tells us that Abel brought the best he had to God. But, on the other hand, nothing is said about the quality of the produce that comprised Cain's offering, just that he brought some of his produce. This seems to imply that, unlike his brother, Cain kept the best for himself and gave God second-rate produce, or the leftovers.

This reminds me of a story I heard of a woman who said she always saved her used tea bags to send to missionaries. Do not laugh because over the years I have seen the same attitude reflected in clothing drives for missions. Talk to charity workers and they will tell you that some of the clothes received are only fit for the dump.

Some givers are like Abel in that they care enough to send the best. Others are more like Cain in that they donate things that are worn out or torn, clothes that should be used as cleaning rags, not gifts for needy people. If we are to enjoy our giving and make our Lord proud of our gifts, we should be more like Abel. Whenever we give to God or to others in His Name we should sacrifice and give the best, symbolic of our understanding of the fact that when God gave His only Son for us, He gave us His best! So, a good question for us to ask ourselves is this: "When it comes to my offerings, am I more like Abel or Cain?"

Third: what they chose to offer

Cain brought the fruit of the ground but Abel brought the fruit of the flock. One brother brought vegetation. The other brought animal life. In my mind this is the main reason Cain's offering was rejected. God had already begun to teach them that the purpose of these offerings was to atone for sin and that atonement for sin required a substitute. Something had to die, a life for a life. Do you remember that in the Garden of Eden, an apron of leaves was insufficient to cover Adam and Eve's shame? So in Genesis 3:23 we read *that God provided them with animal skins, implying the death of an animal.*

By the same token, the fruit of the ground was insufficient to cover Cain's sin and both Cain and his brother would have known this. Their parents would have told them. In fact, I believe God Himself would have told them. Referring to the first set of clothes, God told Adam and Eve that they needed to understand that sin was no little thing. God used these skins as the first of many object lessons down through the centuries to help them and their descendants realise that sin leads to death and because it does, a sinless victim must die in order that sinners might be pardoned. Even these first sacrifices pointed forward to Christ, the spotless Lamb of God who would come to die on the cross. In that one sacrificial act, He would take our sins on Himself. So, when Abel came with a *slain innocent lamb, whose blood had been shed,* he was honouring God's instructions. Like a rebellious pupil, Cain's proud offering showed that he ignored them. If nothing else, the record of God rejecting Cain's offering should remind us that:

> "Without the shedding of blood there is no forgiveness."
> Hebrews 9:22.

That is why Jesus came. He did not come to Earth just to teach us good things. No, He came to die, to shed His precious blood for us because that was the price of atoning for our sins and God loved us too much not to pay it.

Genesis 4 verse 7 says that God patiently, graciously gave Cain a second chance to get his offering right and he could have done so. Cain could have traded some of his produce for one of his brother's lambs and sacrificed it. His arrogance and conceit prevented him from doing so. Instead he became angry enough to want his brother dead, angry enough to act on that desire and lure his brother into the fields where he, the first child born committed the first murder, a premeditated, cold-blooded killing.

God of course knew what had happened. His eyes see all things. His mind knows all thoughts. In His grace He gave Cain a chance to confess his crime by asking, "Cain, where is your brother?" This brings us to this chapter's question, as Cain sarcastically replies *"How should I know? Am I my brother's keeper?"* What is the answer to the first recorded question by a member of the human race? Was Cain responsible for not only his brother's death but also his life?

I think the answer to that question is obvious but it brings other questions to my inquiring mind:

- Are we our brothers' keepers?
- Are you and I responsible for the needs of other people?

What do you think? Are you and I obligated to help those who are in need? There are both material and spiritual needs in this world that has been devastated by sin. You know the problems as well as I do and I ask you:

- Is it our job to feed the hungry and to clothe the poor?
- Do we owe anything to the downtrodden, the orphans and the widows?
- Is it our job to minister to the sick?
- Are other people's problems our problem?
- If Christians engage in sin, is it our job to speak to them? Are we responsible for helping to guide them away from their sin and back to righteous living?

I am sorry if these questions overwhelm you but the answer to every question is yes. As Christians we are indeed our brothers' and sisters' keepers!

Let me point out two basic facts that underscore this truth:

- God's Word teaches it.
- Our witness depends on it.

First: God's Word teaches it

- The clear teaching of the Bible is that we are our brother's keeper:

    "Religion that God our Father accepts as pure and faultless

is this: to look after orphans and widows in their distress." James 1:27.

"Anyone who does not do what is right is not a child of God; nor is anyone who does not love his brother...If anyone has material possessions and sees his brother in need but has no pity on him, how can the love of God be in him?"
1 John 3:10,

"let us not love with words or tongue but with actions and in truth." 1 John 3:17 & 18.

If we see a brother or sister without clothes or food ...and do nothing about his physical needs ...our faith is a dead faith, we are told in James 2:15-17.

❑ God approves of people whose faith in Him moves them to:

"...loose the chains of injustice...set the oppressed free...share your food with the hungry...provide the poor wanderer with shelter...when you see the naked, to clothe him..." Isaiah 58:6 - 7.

❑ We could go on because God:

"...defends the cause of the fatherless and the widow and loves the alien, giving him food and clothing."
Deuteronomy 10:18.

As His children, God calls us to do the same. Think of it this way. As Christians, our business is to do God's business and God's business is people! Whenever we see a brother in need, what we are really seeing is God inviting us to join Him in His work. So, whenever we come across a person in need we must realise this is a Divine appointment! God is calling us to join Him in doing what is primary in His heart and help people.

The movie, *The Four Feathers* is the story of a British soldier who, rather than go to war, resigns his commission. His friends are shocked and show their belief that he is a coward by each sending him a white feather, which was the customary way to convey this message back then. Later in the film, this so called coward learns that his friends are in trouble on the battlefield and he risks his own life and travels to Africa to come to their aid. In the process of tracking down his friends he is stranded in the desert dying of thirst. A native of that country comes across his unconscious body and nurses him back to health. Then he actually assists him in his quest to help his friends. In spite of the bad treatment the native had experienced over and over again because of his race, he risks his own life to help. And, at the end of the film he is asked why he has done this. Why has this stranger made someone else's business his own? His reply is very moving. He says, "I did this because God put you in my way." In his mind, perceived human need was the same thing as God's command to help.

Fellow Christian, the Bible teaches that we too should embrace this philosophy. Whenever we see a need that we can meet we must realise God is calling us to meet it. When God puts needy, lonely, hungry, fearful, sick and unsaved people in our way, He is telling us to go to their aid. Unfortunately when faced with human need, many look the other way. Many look for an excuse not to help.

It reminds me of the story about the comic W. C. Fields. Toward the end of his life when he was bedridden and dying, a friend stopped by to see him and was surprised to find him reading his Bible. This friend knew that Fields had no love for the Christian faith so he asked him, "Why in the world are you reading the Bible? Are you looking for answers?" Fields replied, "No, I am looking for loopholes."

When many of us read Jesus' command for us to lay our lives down for our brothers in the same selfless way that He laid His life down for us, we too look for loopholes.

Like the religious people in Jesus' parable of the Good Samaritan, when we encounter someone in need we tend to look for excuses to pass by on the other side. We give lots of reasons for doing this but I think the most popular excuse is that we are already worn out trying to take care of ourselves and we just want a break. We do not want to get more tired than we already are. Well, my first response to people who think this way is to ask: *"Where do we get the idea that Christians are supposed to be well-rested?"* The Bible does not teach that, in fact, it teaches that we are here to work. As Jesus said:

"As long as it is day, we must do the work of Him Who sent Me. Night is coming, when no one can work." John 9:4.

In other words, rest comes later. Comfort is what Heaven, not Earth, is all about. We are here in this world to do God's work. As I said, God's work and God's business is people. This life of ours is not a holiday. Heaven is the holiday. That is when we move into the mansions that God has prepared for us. Here and now in this sinful world of which we are temporary residents, Christians should get tired! We can rest later! When we join God in His work of helping the needy, we will expend our time, money and energy. That is the way it should be on this side of eternity.

C. S. Lewis once said: *"The only place outside of Heaven where you can be perfectly safe from all the dangers of love is hell."* He is right! It is dangerous to love. It is tiring, costly even but that is what we are here for. The ironic thing is that when we give and continue to give all we are and have to help people, only then do we truly begin to live! That is because we are living as we should live. That is when life gets exciting!

The main reason Jesus calls us to a life of service is not

just because other people need our service. It is because of what happens to us when we serve. When we deny self and join God in His work by helping others, we truly begin to experience an abundant quality of life. This is because when we help the people God puts in our way, He provides us with His presence, strength and resources. So, whenever we see a needy person and pass by on the other side, we are not just passing by that person, we are passing by a chance to literally work side-by-side with Almighty God! We are passing by a taste of Paradise, a chance to walk with God in His work, just as Adam and Eve walked with Him in the Garden of Eden.

So, we must be our brothers' keeper because God's Word teaches it and

Second: our WITNESS depends on it

Not only are we responsible for people's physical needs, we are also responsible for providing their spiritual needs. As Christians it is our job to join our Lord, not just in feeding and clothing the poor but also in seeking and saving the lost. And the fact is, people will not listen to us tell them about God's sacrificial love until we sacrificially act to help them. To them, our willingness to get our hands dirty and become involved in their needs is evidence of our personal experience with a loving God. Somehow our unsaved friends sense that as 1 John 3:14 says, Christians show that they are Christians when they show that they:

"...have passed from death to life..."

"...love other people."   1 John 3:14

As Martin Luther observed: *"Faith alone justifies, yet faith is never alone. It is never without love. If love is lacking, neither is there faith but mere hypocrisy."* Loving our neighbours and the giving of ourselves to help them is indeed visible evidence of our relationship to God.

A lady tells of engaging in a conversation with two couples, one Christian and one Buddhist. About halfway through the conversation, one of the Christians lit up a cigarette and apologised saying he was trying to give them up because he knew they hurt his testimony. The Buddhist woman immediately interjected, "Do not worry about it. You see when one of our ranks becomes a Christian, we do not watch them to see how well they live up to some self-imposed standard of piety. We watch them to see how they start treating people."

People do watch us because the truth is that we often have to earn the right to share our faith. The way we earn it is by living it. The way we should live it is by "keeping our brothers", selflessly loving and caring for others. We need to get this right. We want to respond as Abel did by giving God our best and coming to Him in the right attitude. Ask yourself:

Question 1. What do I need to give to God?

Question 2. Is God calling me to join a church group where I can offer Him my time and talents to be used in ministry to the hurting and lost people of this world?

Question 3. Does my attitude towards all the needy people around me, my neighbours and co-workers, even beggars who I avoid in the street, need to change?

You need to say, God I want to respond by giving my time and all my resources to help these people. I want to join You in Your work.

Chapter 2   Genesis 22:1-19

Where is The Lamb?

We are familiar with times of testing because life is full of tests of various kinds. One of the best ways to prepare for a test is to study previous ones. Many places of education make previous exam papers available to their current students as a way of helping them to understand the type of questions that will be asked them. In this chapter we study the way Abraham responded to a test he had to endure. I believe that if we study the way he handled this time of testing, it will help us to be prepared when we face tests in our own lives. Let us look at the text surrounding the question in Genesis 22.

"Some time later God tested Abraham. He said to him, "Abraham!" "Here I am," he replied. Then God said, "Take your son, your only son, Isaac, whom you love, and go to the region of Moriah. Sacrifice him there as a burnt offering on one of the mountains I will tell you about." Early the next morning Abraham got up and saddled his donkey. He took with him two of his servants and his son Isaac. When he had cut enough wood for the burnt offering, he set out for the place God had told him about. On the third day, Abraham looked up and saw the place in the distance. He said to his servants, "Stay here with the donkey while I and the boy go over there. We will worship and then we will come back to you." Abraham took the wood for the burnt offering and placed it on his son Isaac, and he himself carried the fire and the knife. As the two of them went on together, Isaac spoke up and said to his father, Abraham, "Father?" "Yes, my son?" Abraham replied. "The fire and wood are here," Isaac said, "but where is the lamb for the burnt offering?" Abraham answered, "God Himself will provide the lamb for the burnt offering, my son." And the two of them went on together. When they reached the place God had told him about, Abraham built an altar there and arranged the wood on it. He bound his son Isaac and laid him on the altar, on top of the wood. Then he reached out his hand and took the knife to slay his son. But the angel of the Lord called out to him from heaven, "Abraham, Abraham!" "Here I am," he replied. "Do not lay a hand on the boy," he said. "Do not do anything to him. Now I know that you fear God, because you have not withheld from me your son, your only son." Abraham looked up and there in a thicket he saw a ram caught by its horns. He went over and took the ram and sacrificed it as a burnt offering instead of his son. So Abraham called that place, "The Lord Will Provide." And to this day it is said, "on the mountain of the Lord it will be provided." The angel of the LORD called to Abraham from heaven a second time and said, "I swear by myself, declares the LORD, that because you have done this and have not withheld your son, your only son, I will surely bless you and make your descendants as numerous as the stars in the sky and as the sand on the seashore. Your descendants will take possession of the cities of their enemies, and through your offspring all nations on earth will be blessed, because you have obeyed me." Then Abraham returned to his servants, and they set off together for Beersheba. And Abraham stayed in Beersheba." Genesis 22:1-19.

How did Abraham respond to this time of testing? We learn how testing can:

- Reveal the true nature of faith.
- Strengthen faith in God's promises.
- Reveal the true nature of love.

First: testing reveals the true nature of faith

Let us go back a little way and you will see why I say this. At the very beginning of his walk with God, our Heavenly

Father told Abraham that he would be the father of a great and mighty nation. God had repeated and even enlarged on this promise several times in Abraham's life and as a way of confirming this pledge, God had even changed his name from Abram, which means, "father of many" to Abraham which means, "Father of a great multitude." However, in all those years from Abraham's early seventies, when he first received this promise, to when he was 99 years old, the small company of his immediate family had shrunk instead of growing towards "nation-sized status":

- His father Terah died.
- Lot abandoned him and took his family to live near Sodom.
- Ishmael and his mother Hagar had been sent away.

So Abraham's family had got less like a multitude every day. But in spite of this Abraham still believed God. He trusted God to keep His word. Finally, when Abraham was 99 years old, nearly a quarter of a century since God first gave him this promise, He sent three angelic visitors to Abraham. They said that within the year Sarah would give birth to his son, a statement that made the aged Sarah laugh. She knew her childbearing years had long since passed. The angel's message turned out to be true because that is exactly what happened. A son was born to them when Abraham was 100 years old and Sarah 90 and in accordance with God's specific instructions, they named this child of promise Isaac.

Perhaps on the evening of the day of Isaac's miraculous birth, as Sarah and Isaac slept, Abraham walked out of his tent, looked up at the sky, saw countless stars and remembered God's promise recorded in Genesis 15:5 that:

"...his offspring would be as numerous as the countless number of lights in the night sky." Genesis 15:5.

Little Isaac grew as did the love and pride Abraham felt for him. I am sure those first years were full of celebrations. Genesis 21 tells us that Abraham's entire clan had a feast to celebrate Isaac being weaned from his mother and at that feast God confirmed to Abraham once again that it would be through Isaac that His promise would be fulfilled. Yes, that Isaac would marry, have a family and from that family, from Abraham's lineage, the promised Deliverer would come, the Redeemer that every one since Adam and Eve had been longing for.

Our reading tells us that Abraham did as God asked. He instructed his two servants to spend the night gathering everything they would need for the journey. Then the next morning, as soon as there was enough light to travel, he took his son, the two servants, plus enough wood for the sacrifice and headed out in the direction of Mount Moriah waiting for God's promised specific guidance when he got there. Abraham responded in the same way as he had done when God first called him to leave his homeland of Ur. Then, he left home not knowing exactly where he was to go. In his response to this test Abraham shows us authentic faith. Authentic faith is seen in an obedience that is fuelled by an accurate understanding of the nature and character of God. A. W. Tozer said: *"what we think about God is the most important thing about us."*

Our knowledge of God influences how we respond to His commands. Based on his knowledge of God, Abraham obeyed. Even though he did not understand the command, he obeyed because of his understanding of God. Hebrews gives an insight into Abraham's response when it says he:

"...reasoned that God could raise the dead." Hebrews 11:19.

Abraham had enough faith in God to expect the resurrection of his son. Abraham's walk with God, many years of experiencing God and getting to know Him, had given him this understanding. In fact, I imagine that as he thought about God's terrifying command and decided how to respond to it, Abraham reviewed the things that he had learned about God over the past twenty-five years.

His thought process was perhaps something like this:

- *God is not a liar. I know that! He is truth itself and He has always acted in truth with me. The God of truth has promised that Isaac will be the man through whom His promise to me and to all humanity will be fulfilled. His promise cannot change.*
- *Not only is God not a liar, He cannot be mistaken. After all, He told me that I would have a son in my old age and I did. I mean, when I should have been walking into a retirement home, I walked into the maternity ward! So Isaac must survive this ordeal or God could be mistaken and He never has been.*
- *Experience has also taught me that God is love. Why, He is always worked for my good! He is always acted out of love toward me, even when I have failed Him!*

Let me condense my thoughts:

- *God is truth.*
- *God keeps His word.*
- *God cannot be mistaken.*
- *God has always acted out of love toward me.*
- *God commands me to put Isaac to death.*

Now this last thing seems to contradict the other four but

I know that:

- *There is no contradiction in God.*
- *I have only seen majesty and wisdom in God, never any weaknesses like contradictions.*
- *God knows all about me and controls everything for my earthly and eternal blessing.*

And what about the tremendous power that I have seen Him use? What an all-powerful God He is. Think of those things I have seen Him do:

- *Look what He did to Sodom and Gomorrah.*
- *Look what He did in me! God resurrected in me, an old man of 100 years, the ability to father a child and in Sarah, the ability to conceive and carry the child, although she was 90 years old at the time. God can make the impossible possible! As He once said to me:*

> 'Is anything too hard for the Lord?' Genesis 18:14.

- *No! God can do anything!*

To sum up. I believe that God is truth, He cannot be mistaken, He is love and there is no contradiction in Him. He is all-powerful. Isaac will live. God will resurrect him. I will obey.

All of Abraham's first-hand knowledge of God, gleaned from his many years of experience with God, led him to conclude that he was about to see yet another miracle. We can see this in verse 5. As he and Isaac headed up the mountain he instructs the servants to stay put and added:

> "... *we* will worship and then *we* will come back to you!"
> Genesis 22:5.

In order for us to endure the inevitable trials and tribulations of life, we need to develop this kind of faith as well. We can if we learn and then embrace an understanding of God's nature and character. We get this accurate understanding by reading His Word and reviewing the way God has always interacted with people like Abraham.

We must also follow Abraham's example and look back at our own lives and review all the things God has done for us. Things that show us what He is like. I challenge you to do that. Think:

- Has God always been truthful to you?
- Has God kept His promises to guide you through life and empower you to do His will?
- Have you felt God's presence in fearful lonely times when you prayed?
- Has God been faithful to provide you with your needs?

Let me add my own testimony. God has always acted toward me just as He promises in His Word. He has forgiven me. He has helped me over and over again in so many ways. I have felt His presence. As He has promised, I have found Him to be:

> "An ever present help in time of trouble." Psalm 46:1.

God has been completely faithful and loving toward me in the past, so I believe He will be completely faithful and loving toward me in the future. For this reason, I cannot sing one of my favourite hymns, "Great is Thy faithfulness..." without feeling it deeply. God's faithfulness is indeed great. In fact, that is an understatement. We all need total faith in God's great faithfulness. Until we rest in God and have an accurate understanding of God that fuels our faith, we will never attempt great things for Him.

Hudson Taylor, founder of the China Inland Mission used to hang a plaque in his home with two Hebrew Names on it. "Ebenezer" and "Jehovah Jireh"

- Ebenezer means, "Hitherto hath the Lord helped us".
- Jehovah Jireh means "the Lord will see to it or provide in the future."

One Name looks back while the other looks forward. One reminded Taylor of God's faithfulness in the past and the other of God's promise to be faithful to him in the future. This conviction enabled Taylor to risk everything in God's work of seeking and saving the lost in China. In so doing, he founded the modern missionary movement.

Second: Testing strengthens our faith in God's promises

We see this in the name that Abraham called that place:

"The Lord Will Provide." Genesis 22:14.

Abraham expressed his faith that someday another child would be born. This child would come from his lineage and He would be the long-awaited Deliverer. So, the way he "answered" this test teaches us the true nature of faith. It reminds us that authentic faith is seen in obedience. Abraham's experience can help us to learn one more thing.

Third: It teaches us the true nature of love

Abraham's obedience not only showed his faith. It also showed the depth of his love for God. As 1 John says:

"This is love for God, to obey His commands." 1 John 5:3.

We also see the love of God for both Abraham and ourselves in this event. When we think of our love for God, never forget that that He loved us before we ever loved Him. This event in Genesis 22 foretold Jesus' obedience when, in love to His Father and us, He laid down His life for us on the Cross of Calvary. 1 John also says,

"This is how we know what love is: Jesus Christ laid down his life for us." 1John 3:16

This entire time of testing for Abraham was really an object lesson designed to point to Jesus' sacrifice on our behalf and we see that in the numerous ways that Isaac's life and experience paralleled that of Jesus.

Let me review the similarities and you will see what I mean.

First, they were both:

- Promised sons.
- Born miraculously:
  - Jesus was born of a virgin
  - Isaac was born of a woman well past her childbearing years.
- Born at a time that was accurately predicted by angelic messengers.
- Sons who brought joy to their fathers.
- Obedient to death:
  - Jesus: He "humbled himself and became obedient to death — even death on a cross!" Philippians 2:8.
  - Isaac: He was old enough and strong enough to have resisted his father who was over 100 years old

but he did not because he was obedient.

Second, we read about the two sacrifices:

- Genesis 22:2. God told Abraham to take, "his only son...whom he loved..." to be sacrificed.
- John 3:16. God sent... "His only son..." Whom He loved to be sacrificed for our sins.

Remember that Abraham was to sacrifice Isaac on Mount Moriah and this was the mountain on which Jerusalem was eventually built. Scholars tell us that Abraham's sacrifice was in close proximity to where Jesus was crucified as the final sacrifice.

Third, two resurrections are foretold:

- Abraham said to the servants, "We will come to you..."
- Prior to His crucifixion Jesus told His disciples, "I will come to you."

The letter to the Hebrews also mentions this parallel saying that figuratively speaking:

> "Abraham.....did receive Isaac back from death."
> Hebrews 11:19.

So, there are many parallels between what happened in Genesis 22 and what happened during first Holy Week in Jerusalem when Jesus:

"was delivered over to death for our sins and was raised to life for our justification" Romans 4:25.

Having looked at some parallels, I want you to note that it is important we fully appreciate:

A very important difference

- Abraham did not have to go through with the sacrifice of his son.
- God did go through with the sacrifice of His Son.

F. B. Meyer said: *"So long as men live in the world, they will turn to this story [in Genesis 22] with un-waning interest. There is only one scene in history by which it is surpassed: that scene in which the Great Father gave His 'Isaac' to a death from which there was no deliverance."*

So in sending Abraham to sacrifice his son on Mount Moriah, God foretold the day when He would send His own Son to die as a sacrifice for the sins of all mankind. In essence, Isaac's question, "Where is the lamb?" continued to be asked for hundreds of years by various prophets and hopeful people until the day dawned when a Man from Galilee came to the lower end of the Jordan River to be baptised by a prophet who had been turning the countryside upside down by his preaching. The prophet's name was John the Baptist. Remember what he said when he saw Jesus.

"Look! [there is] the Lamb of God Who takes away the sin of the world!" John 1:29.

When we consider the words of Abraham to Isaac recorded in Genesis 22: 8, we know that in due time, "God Himself" did provide the Lamb. He loved us enough to send "His only Son whom He loved" to die in our place. As Hebrews says, the animal sacrifices made for centuries, were just a:

"reminder of sins. Christ came into the world because it is

impossible for the blood of bulls and goats to take away sins." Hebrews 10:3-4.

Jesus loved us enough to come into the world and to be obedient even to death on the cross. We remind ourselves of this as we take communion! With these symbolic elements we celebrate what Abraham proclaimed on that mountain so long ago. God Himself did indeed provide the Lamb!

What do we learn from God's test of Abraham?

We learn that God tests his children. Abraham is not the only child of God who has been tested. We can see from The Bible that throughout history, God has tested His children. He tested Job, Peter and Paul and God is *still* testing His children! God tests His best. It is never with a desire to see whether we will fail. God's desire is that we pass the test and move on to the next level in spiritual living. If you are really trying to grow as a Christian, trying to give the best of your commitment to Jesus Christ and trying to surrender all that you have and all that you are to God, be ready! God is going to test you.

Abraham did not know it was a test. Job and the others never knew that they were being tested. When God tests us, we seldom know it is a test. All we know is that we find ourselves in some kind of predicament. God might say to us: "Give up what is most precious to you." God said to Abraham: "I want you to give up your only son, the son whom you love." Can you imagine a more difficult command than that? The natural response would be, "Oh God! Anything but that!" Because Abraham trusted God he was willing to do whatever God told him to do. During our testing, we must trust God too! The hymn writer, Rev. J.

H. Sammis explained this truth when he wrote these now famous words:

*"Trust and obey, for there is no other way
To be happy in Jesus, but to trust and obey."*

Do we want to "be happy in Jesus"? If so, trust must come before obedience. We will never be obedient if we lack trust. Abraham trusted God's plan and we need to trust God's plan for us too.

I confess that sometimes when God tells me to do something I have the terrible tendency to want to say, "WHY? or why do I have to do it that way? Is not there some other way?" We get in trouble when we try to exchange God's plan for our own plan because we think that God's plan does not make sense. It did not make any sense for a man to kill his only son when God had promised that he would have descendants more numerous than the stars and the sands of the sea did it? Many of the commands of God in His Word do not make sense from a human standpoint. If you are only going to obey the commands that you can figure out, or only obey those plans that you think make sense, you will not obey very many of them. Abraham trusted God's plan.

Imagine Isaac is 16. Do not most of you think that a 16-year-old could have overpowered a 116-year-old man? When Isaac was about to be tied up with rope and laid on the altar, do not you think a 16-year-old could have said,

"Stop, father. What are you doing?"

It was not only Abraham who trusted God's plan. Isaac was also a willing sacrifice.

Always remember in regard to Jesus that:

- He was not murdered.
- He was not a martyr to a cause that He believed in.
- He willingly laid down his life.
- That was God's plan for Him, His only Son, all along.

Abraham was so certain of God's plan that he said to the servants *"We are going to come back to you."*

Some struggle with this story of Abraham and Isaac and wonder how:

- Abraham could have been willing to sacrifice his only son.
- A loving God could command it.

There is an easy answer to these questions in Hebrews 11:

"By faith Abraham, when God tested him, offered Isaac as a sacrifice. He who had received the promises was about to sacrifice his one and only son. Even though God had said to him, "It is through Isaac that your offspring will be reckoned." Abraham reasoned that God could raise the dead, and figuratively speaking, he did raise Isaac back from death." Hebrews 11:17-19.

When Abraham laid Isaac on the altar, tied him down and took the knife, Isaac was as good as dead! God said "Stop!" Abraham released Isaac. It was as if God had brought him back from the dead.

Take it one step further back. Abraham had so much faith in God and God's promise that he believed that even if he killed Isaac, God was going to raise Isaac from the dead on the spot. Abraham believed God so much he thought, *"If I cut the throat of my son and he bleeds until his heart stops beating, until he is stone cold dead, God is going to raise him back from the dead and both of us are going to walk down that mountain and return to the servants. And God is going to keep His promise!"*

That is faith!

Abraham had faith in God's provision

That is why Abraham named the place where he built the altar, "Jehovah Jireh", which means, our God will provide! We throw that Name around, do not we? We think of God's Provision. We buy provisions. God provides. *Provide* comes from two Latin words *pro,* meaning "before" and *video,* meaning, "I see".

The word "provide" means to *see before what is needed.* In other words when the Bible says, God provides for you and provides for me, it means God sees in advance what we need. We really do not know what we need but God does. He can see what we need before we need it! That is what it means. God provides for our needs.

Isaac, being an inquisitive young man said, "I see the fire. I see the wood but where is the lamb?" Abraham said

"God will provide a lamb."

The Provision of The Lamb

There are three points concerning God's provision of a lamb that you can connect starting with Isaac's question, "Where is the lamb?" in Genesis 22.

First - The cry of HISTORY.

The question of the Old Testament, "Where is the lamb?"

Second - The cry of HOLINESS.

Thousands of years later, John the Baptist answered Isaac's question. John pointed his finger to Jesus as Jesus commenced his public ministry and John said:
"Look, the Lamb of God, who takes away the sin of the world." John 1:29.

Jesus, the sinless Lamb of God, died for us on the cross.

Third - The cry of HEAVEN

In Revelation 5 we read that all the redeemed of all the ages will be gathered around the Throne of God and we are going to sing "a new song" to the Lamb of God. "You are worthy ..." Revelation 5:9. We will also hear the angels sing: "Worthy is the Lamb who was slain..." Revelation 5:12. God's Word is so wonderful in the way the theme runs from beginning to end:

- Genesis: "Where is the Lamb"?
- Gospel of John: "Behold the Lamb."
- Revelation: "Worthy is the Lamb".

Our God is the God who provides. He sees what we need and He provides for that need.

Dr. John Phillips wrote one short paragraph about this in his commentary on Genesis: "Was there ever such a dark, tragic work performed beneath the wide vault of heaven in all the ages of time or all the annals of eternity? God saw his only son led like a lamb to the slaughter, laid out upon the wood and the spikes driven home. God watched the whole dark, dreadful business on Golgotha's Hill not far from Moriah. Then, God himself had taken the great knife of his own fierce wrath against sin and had lifted it up as the darkness swept in and had wreaked on his son the eternal hell that our sins deserve. That was the work of the cross. The work that was enacted in type by Abraham on that lonely mountain in the land of Moriah and enacted in fact at the place called Calvary."

It makes us glad that when Abraham was about to kill his son, God said "Stop! You do not have to kill your son. Here is a substitute" When God's only Son climbed perhaps the very same mountain, there was no substitute. He was the substitute for us. As Isaiah says:

"And God has laid upon him the iniquities of us all." Isaiah 53:6.

Jehovah Jireh is still Jehovah Jireh. God not only provided Abraham with a substitute for Isaac, He provided Jesus as a substitute for you and me. So when you are tested, trust Him. Trust God's plan and trust God's provision.

Great blessings result from obedience

In Genesis 22:15-18, we read that God repeated to Abraham the promise He had received concerning his descendants being as numerous as the stars and the sands of the sea. Additionally, God promised Abraham that all the people of the Earth were going to be blessed. The reason God gave to Abraham for this additional promise:

"Because you have obeyed me". Genesis 22:18.

When you are tested and you trust and obey, God will bless your obedience too. You say, "Well that is a great Old Testament story. Does the New Testament talk about that?" Read what James says:

"Blessed is the man who perseveres under trial, because when he has stood the test, he will receive the crown of life that God has promised to those who love him." James 1:12.

Is God calling upon you to go to a new place or to give up something that is precious to you and you do not know what is going on? Do not worry! It could be that God is testing you and He wants you to trust and obey. When you pass the test, you will graduate to the next grade and God will test you again. You will be blessed as you continue to obey.

Chapter 3   Psalm 73

Who Have I In Heaven But You?

All Christians at some time questioned what they believe. One could argue that those who say that they do not are either dishonest or unintelligent. The only faith immune from doubt is *blind faith,* which deserves to be called a *crutch.* Real faith is not blind and it does not shut its eyes. It cannot. It must deal with reality to be real. Someone reading my words may well be asking: "Have I been wasting my life being a Christian? Is it worth it?"

There is no better example of this dilemma than Psalm 73. The writer has almost slipped from his faith. Life has crumbled away for him. Life has handed him a raw deal. We look at the question asked by Asaph, "Whom have I in heaven but you?" Let us look at the text surrounding it:

"Surely God is good to Israel, to those who are pure in heart. But as for me, my feet had almost slipped; I had nearly lost my foothold. For I envied the arrogant when I saw the prosperity of the wicked. They have no struggles; their bodies are healthy and strong. They are free from the burdens common to man; they are not plagued by human ills. Therefore pride is their necklace; they clothe themselves with violence. From their callous hearts comes iniquity; the evil conceits of their minds know no limits. They scoff, and speak with malice; in their arrogance they threaten oppression. Their mouths lay claim to heaven, and their tongues take possession of the earth. Therefore their people turn to them and drink up waters in abundance. They say, "How can God know? Does the Most High have knowledge?" This is what the wicked are like—always carefree, they increase in wealth. Surely in vain have I kept my heart pure; in vain have I washed my hands in innocence. All day long I have been plagued; I have been punished every morning. If I had said, "I will speak thus," I would have betrayed your children. When I tried to understand all this, it was oppressive to me till I entered the sanctuary of God; then I understood their final destiny. Surely you place them on slippery ground; you cast them down to ruin. How suddenly are they destroyed, completely swept away by terrors! As a dream when one awakes, so when you arise, O Lord, you will despise them as fantasies. When my heart was grieved and my spirit embittered, I was senseless and ignorant; I was a brute beast before you. Yet I am always with you; you hold me by my right hand. You guide me with your counsel, and afterward you will take me into glory. Whom have I in heaven but you? And earth has nothing I desire besides you. My flesh and my heart may fail, but God is the strength of my heart and my portion forever. Those who are far from you will perish; you destroy all who are unfaithful to you. But as for me, it is good to be near God. I have made the Sovereign LORD my refuge; I will tell of all your deeds." Psalm 73.

The question in verse 25 comes riding on the back of a great frustration that we read about in verse 11. Asaph is looking around at people who have little or no time for God and yet seem to have an easier life than those who give God His rightful place in their lives. These people say, "How can God know? Does the Most High have knowledge?" The implication is *No, He does not and He is indifferent to what is going on anyway.*

In Psalm 73 Asaph had nearly lost his foothold. When reading this Psalm we must remember that we are not talking about an ordinary person. By no means. It was Asaph, the worship leader for King David. Asaph was a great composer of music. He could take David's poetry and put it to music and do a brilliant job with it. He wrote memorable tunes that the Jewish Nation enjoyed singing. However, this Psalm is one of his own poems that he set to music and it is pretty tough stuff. He is taking a hard look at life and not liking what he sees. But, his testimony at the end of his Psalm is stronger than ever. He can say about God:

"I will tell of all your deeds." Psalm 73:28.

Let us trace the process of Asaph's struggle from his thoughts of GIVING UP to his decision to keep GOING ON. He did three things:

- He looked around and took stock.
- He looked inward.
- He looked up to God.

HE LOOKED AROUND and took stock

Probably every week Asaph led congregations in songs. I can imagine him saying, "Let us bring our praise to our Lord, people. He is worthy, Amen! Amen! Surely God is good to Israel, to those who are pure in heart. Let us sing"

But Asaph's experience did not square up with the words of the songs. He saw that those who were "proud, arrogant, carefree and indifferent to God" were in better shape than those who were pure in heart. Their way of life did not seem to create a cloud of gloom over their heads. Asaph saw quite the opposite. In the first half of this Psalm he hits on three things regarding these people.

- Prosperity
- Pride
- Popularity.

Asaph is left asking himself the question. "Is it worth it? This God business, what is the point of it?" Do you know what I like about this man? He does not shy away from honesty. Many of our prayers are pointless because we pretend with God. If your boss at work asks you how you are, you tell him that you are fine because you know that your boss does not really want to know about your problems. But it is foolish to behave like that with God. He does want to know about your problems. In fact, He knows about them already but He wants to you to speak to Him about them because He wants you to experience His presence and His peace.

My sympathies go out to the little boy unfairly overlooked for a prize at school. His mother told him that it is an unjust world where virtue is triumphant only in theatricals. It appears that way. I remember seeing an episode of the TV Quiz 'The Weakest Link'. One of the competitors was a vicar. In one round he did not do at all well. The sarcasm of the quiz-mistress just oozed as he was asked "Has God gone on holiday?" I guess you have to expect that sort of comment if you go in for such a quiz. But when you feel it is true in real life that is hard to take. You may at this moment be thinking along these lines: "Okay, it is a problem but what is new? This kind of thing has been happening from our school days. Why should Asaph suddenly be upset because there are people around indifferent to God; without struggles; their bodies healthy and strong, they have proud callous hearts, they are conceited, malicious, always carefree, and they increase in wealth?" What does Asaph do next?

HE LOOKED INWARD

In Verse 13 Asaph wondered whether keeping himself in God's good books has been in vain. He said in verse 14:

"All day long I have been plagued; I have been punished every morning." Psalm 73:14.

The French have a saying *"We are strong enough to bear the ills of others"*. How true! It is our *own* maladies that really get to us. You will understand what the person was getting at who said: "The smallest pain in my little finger creates more mental anguish than the destruction of the thousands of people I see on the TV news." We know it should not be like that but it often is. And when Asaph was *personally* touched he lost his foothold. We read of children killed in war and we get upset. Something should be done. However, if they were our children we would get much more upset. It is tough being unemployed. It would be even tougher if it were you or me! Obviously something has brought this home to Asaph.

To his credit, Asaph did not want to become a stumbling block to anyone else. This added to his problem. He says:

"If I had said, "I will speak thus," I would have betrayed this generation of your children." Psalm 73:15.

We ought to think twice before we give voice to problems. It could damage the people around us who look to us for support. Are your sympathies with Asaph?

- Is a raw deal eating away at you right now?
- Are you struggling with life not being fair?
- Have you pushed angry feelings so far down that you deny they exist?

Or have you already turned from God because you have suffered wrongs? Perhaps they are wrongs inflicted by Christians. Now, as Asaph did, you question God's goodness, character and faithfulness.

Let me make this clear. You are not an unbeliever because you talk like this.

- *Doubt* is not the opposite of *faith*. That is to confuse *unbelief* with *doubt*.
- Only a believer can experience doubt. You can only doubt what you believe.
- When atheists doubt, they start thinking that God might exist after all!

Like the little boy who said to his atheistic parents, "Do you think God knows we do not believe in Him?" Atheists do not feel disappointed with God because they expect nothing. Those who commit their lives to God expect something and therefore are confused when things do not work out as expected. Asaph did not cease to believe because of his uncertainties. His experiences actually strengthened his faith. To confront your doubts honestly need not weaken your faith. It can make it stronger.

Had Asaph not struggled, he would not have gone to God, at least not with the same desperate searching that we read about here. And had he not gone to God like that, we would not have come to develop so deeply in our understanding of who God is and what life is really all about. We have a harder time passionately seeking God when everything is easy. Throughout all generations, it has so often been in the times of severe testing, that believers have grown in ways they could never have dreamed of.

Asaph has been LOOKING AROUND at others doing pretty well without God. He is been LOOKING INWARD at himself feeling punished every morning. Did Asaph stop at this point? If he had, he would never have found out that there is an answer to the things that were dragging him down. So, when and where did he find the answer? Asaph found the answer when he LOOKED UP to God. The turning point in Asaph's experience is described from verse 17.

He LOOKED UP to God

Spiritual problems like Asaph's are a sign that we need a proper perspective. A lot of our problems arise because we stop the crime movie before it is over. Or we only read part of the book and do not get to the last chapter. We can trace the four steps that Asaph took that brought help to him. I am going to give them to you built on the letters of the word HELP:

- H: House
- E: End
- L: Learnt
- P: Praise

Remember H.E.L.P and let it meets your needs now and in the future when facing a raw deal.

The first word is HOUSE

Asaph's real turning point came when he entered the sanctuary (or the HOUSE) of God. Our turning point will come as we meet with fellow believers as a church. I thank God that He has urged us to meet with other Christians. The writer to the Hebrews knew that things were getting tough for believers in his day. In Hebrews 10:25 he wrote:

> "...not to neglect meeting together..." Hebrews 10:25

We should keep the habit of meeting with one another because that is where we get the encouragement and the support that we need to stop us slipping away. Have you noticed how many times Scripture includes references to our wills? There are times when we feel we cannot worship nor have times of fellowship because:

- We are in the wrong mood.
- We feel hypocritical because we are ashamed of our doubts.

We cannot afford to have our worship and times of fellowship directed by our emotions. Asaph somehow found his way to the 'HOUSE' of God and that is where he began to find help. The same will be true of us. Just looking around at other believers can put strength into us. They have had their trials too. They have struggled and still do. But they are going on. This can help because we can bear one another's burdens. We can inspire one another. This is not the whole solution but it is a vital step.

The next word is END

"I entered the sanctuary of God then I understood their final destiny." Psalm 73:17.

Taking the short term view, you might say, "To go God's way is a waste of time and effort. You come off better without Him." Take the long term view and you see things completely differently. Jesus said in Matthew 7:13-14, in the Sermon on the Mount, travel light on the narrow way and you:

- Limit your baggage.
- Limit the kind of company you keep.
- Limit the things that you do.

The broad way gives you plenty of space and allows you to:

- Travel with lots of baggage.

- Widen the kind of company you keep.
- Expand your activities.

Make no mistake:

- There is a difference in those two "roads of life" or ways of living now.
- A different reception awaits travellers at the ends of these two roads.

One road leads to life, the other to destruction. As a believer, you get your troubles now with none to come in eternity. An unbeliever might be relatively free from troubles now but in eternity they will never cease. You have a bad dream but it ends when you wake up. It was just a dream, not something real and lasting. God sees the prosperity of the wicked as only a dream:

"As a DREAM when one awakes, so when you arise, O Lord, you will despise them as fantasies." Psalm 73:20.

Success and failure must be put in their proper perspective. Once Asaph:

- Came to the 'HOUSE' of God.
- Met with other believers.
- Got the bigger perspective.
- Saw the 'END' awaiting those who are indifferent to God.

He did not want to change places with the unbelievers for anything. The next thing that helped him was that:

He 'LEARNT' something

Asaph did not just feel better he says:

"I understood their final destiny." Psalm 73:17.

If our religion only reaches our feelings it is not really worthwhile. There are many ways of temporarily trying to forget our troubles. Some will:

- Watch a film or television.
- Read.
- Listen to music.
- Foolishly try to drown their troubles in alcohol.

How do we seek to forget our troubles? Does whatever we do help us to reach a spiritual understanding of the problem? We just lose ourselves in our emotions if we do not think about what we are doing. Let me emphase this point. We know that Asaph was the worship leader of Israel. There can be false comfort in singing spiritual songs in church. It could be little different from a singsong at the local pub unless we think about what we are doing and the reason why we are doing it. This ditty just about sums up the approach of some churchgoers:

"I am a Christian in my way,
How? It is difficult to say.
I have the haziest sort of notion
What I mean by my devotion.
Clichés clutter up my head,
Catchwords are my daily bread.
Exquisitely undefined,
Is the thing I call my mind."

Never forget that the message of the Bible is to the mind. One of the satisfying things about Christianity is that we have a reason for our hope. It is vital that we take the time to think about what we are doing. Going to the sanctuary of God for Asaph was not just a shot in the arm or a nice escapism from the real world outside. The sanctuary of God was a place to engage Asaph's mind as well as his emotions. It was a place for him to think about his God and how he related to Him. It was the place to do some relating. This can be hard work. To do it properly may cause you to go home from church more tired than when you arrived! When Asaph entered the sanctuary of God he UNDERSTOOD:

- ❏ The end of the wicked, "their final destiny."
- ❏ That what had led to his problem had been self-induced.

Asaph had built a molehill into a mountain. He is not alone because:

- ❏ I have done this and so have you.
- ❏ We let our feelings dominate us.
- ❏ We do not let the truths about our big eternal God saturate our minds and grip our thinking.

That is why a regular habit of church attendance is good. Once in a place of Christian worship we see ourselves as we really are. As Asaph says to God:

"I was senseless and ignorant; I was a brute beast before you." Psalm 73:22.

Asaph probably never battled with this particular problem again because he worked it through. HELP for doubt comes as we go to God's HOUSE and meet with fellow believers. Do not give up on that. We see the END for those who are full of themselves. Asaph thought that he was in a slippery place. Now, from the standpoint of eternity, he saw that it is the unbelievers that are on 'slippery ground'. How suddenly everything can change. He had LEARNT something. He has thought through his faith and has realised that God's plans are bigger than a few years of success now. He is getting some sense into his attitude. The final thing Asaph does that HELPS is

PRAISE God

Outside the House of God he thought God was being unfair to him. Inside God's house he is PRAISING and that gets him focused on real and lasting values:

> "Yet I am always with you; you hold me by my right hand." Psalm 73:23.

People often say glibly that we should just hold on to the Lord. I am grateful that my relationship is not dependent on my grip of His hand. It is His grip of my hand that counts. When you cross the road with a child, the child holds your hand. But really, it is your grip that counts. Asaph goes on to say:

> "You guide me with your counsel and afterward you will take me into glory." Psalm 73:24.

One day you may pay off your mortgage or get a better car. So what! I pity people whose interest is only in such things. Every car will go to its last rusting place! With the price of current funerals, I am glad to be alive! As for Asaph, his envy has gone. He can now say:

> "Whom have I in heaven but you, and earth has nothing I desire besides you. My flesh and my heart may fail, but God is the strength of my heart and my portion forever." Psalm 73:25-26.

He has fallen in love with God again because he has got a proper focus on the things that matter both now and eternally. Perhaps you know only too well from bitter experience how easy it is to lose the talking side of the relationship in a marriage. It can drift out in your spiritual relationship as well. It must not!

When we love God our questions do not disappear

We would be both foolish and arrogant if we thought that we had or we knew all the answers. Questions may remain with us to our last day. However, they can and must be considered in a spiritual context. Let us recall the things that changed Asaph's doubts into delight in God. There is nothing better to assist our UNDERSTANDING than:

- Being with God's people in His HOUSE. Putting what we see now in the wider context.
- Seeing the END of people who have little or next to no time for God. Knowing that for the Christian, death is just a change of address.
- Using our minds to work out the spiritual answer. LEARNING about our faith.
- Bringing our PRAISE to God because whatever doubts we face, we know that we have His abiding presence for time and eternity. God will hold our hand, guide us and take us to glory.

Look at how Asaph finished his song.

Unbelievers may cynically say:

"How can God know? Does the Most High have knowledge?" Psalm 73:11.

What does Asaph say?

When he concludes Psalm 73, Asaph is no longer fuming

about getting a raw deal.

"Those who are far from you will perish; you destroy all who are unfaithful to you. But as for me, it is good to be near God. I have made the sovereign LORD my refuge; I will tell of all your deeds." Psalm 73:.27-28.

Do not run away from your doubts

Never yield to the schoolboy definition of 'faith' that faith is: 'believing in something that you know is not true'. That is nonsense. Compelling oneself to believe is no part of true religion. We do not give up the quest for truth and become Christians. There is nothing 'unspiritual' about doubts. Learn from Asaph. Look doubt in the face with a better perspective and be stronger because of it.

If you are not sure about what you believe - do not run away from your faith. Some reading this book may have doubts about aspects of Christianity. Do not sweep doubts under a mental carpet as that would be both dishonest and unhelpful. Doubts are not the only things that we have got, are they? Like Asaph, we are aware of God's presence with us. We know that we belong to Him. We know that there is so much more for us to learn about eternal truths and our personal relationship with God. I say, do not run away from what you already know and have experienced to be true. What fantastic blessings you would miss out on if you did.

My many years of experience as both a Christian and a pastor have taught me that when believers read or hear the Word of God preached, there is a response within us that confirms that our Christian faith is both real and genuine.

We are all aware of those who say that they need proof.

What do they mean by proof? Scientific proof?

- Do they think you can put God in a test tube and run experiments on Him?
- Can you measure 'right or wrong' with a ruler?
- Can you measure 'love' with a voltmeter?

Everyone knows that you cannot do these things. And here is the reason why. It is not sufficient just to have knowledge of God's existence.

Experiencing God personally is what really matters.

Take one step toward God and He will take a dozen toward you. This is more than good advice based on many years' personal experience of counselling those who have doubts, because Scripture also confirms it is true. You can bank on it. Do it and you will be able to assist others who need to experience a close personal relationship with God too.

Two men in an art gallery came upon a painting of a chess game entitled Checkmate. One player was a man; the other the Devil. The man was down to his last piece. One of the two men looking at this painting was a chess champion and he became so engrossed that his friend grew impatient and asked him what he was doing. He said, "There is something about this painting that bothers me and I want to study it for a little while. You go ahead and wander around." His head started nodding, and his hands started moving. When his friend came back, he said, "We have to locate the artist and tell him that either he has to change the picture or the title. There is something wrong with this painting." His friend asked, "What?" The man said, "Well, it is titled Checkmate but the King still has one more move."

Maybe you are reading this and humanly speaking, you face a future that alarms you. I have some good news for you:

The King still has one more move.

The King still has one more move

A boy named David is up against a giant named Goliath. David is in trouble. He tries to put on King Saul's armour but Saul is a 52-Long, and David is a 36-Short. David cannot even handle a sword. It looks like Checkmate, but... *The King still has one more move.*

A man named Daniel gets thrown into a den of lions because he refuses to stop praying to God. The lions are hungry. He is in there all night. At the first light of dawn, Darius calls down to him. Daniel tells him that the lions have been put on a "Low Protein Diet" and he is fine, because... *The King still has one more move.*

A man named Moses convinces a nation of oppressed slaves to run away from the Pharaoh, the most powerful man on Earth and his army. Pharaoh sets out after them. The slaves are standing on the shore with the Red Sea in front of them and the greatest army in the world behind them. The people say to Moses, "Moses, what were you thinking"? And Moses says to God, "God, what were You thinking?" The slaves escape on dry land as the Red Sea divided because... *The King still has one more move!*

Going down to Judea to see Lazarus cost Jesus His life, as He knew it would. And they tried Him and judged Him; they whipped Him and beat Him; they mocked Him and scorned Him; they hung Him on a cross to die and laid Him low in a tomb to rot, the way every human body has rotted ever since death entered this sinful world. And then they said to everybody. That's all, folks! Show's over! Time to go home. Checkmate. But they were wrong, because... *The King still has one more move!*

I do not know what challenges you are facing. Maybe there is stress at work or you are in a marriage that is falling apart or one that has already ended. Is there is a son or a daughter, somebody that you love, who is struggling or estranged from you? Do you have financial pressures? Have you done the wrong thing, said the wrong thing or made some other mistake that feels so big it seems unforgivable? Maybe none of life's common problems affect you now but as the mortality rate is still 100%, we all know that no one escapes the consequences of sin. Whatever you face, whether it is today or tomorrow, the promise of Jesus to everyone who puts their trust in Him is this. There is hope, even when it feels like "Checkmate."

Asaph came to know the answer to the great question he asked

Asaph tells us what he has decided to do:

"I have made the Sovereign LORD my refuge." Psalm 73:28.

Decide now to make the Sovereign Lord your continual refuge. Whatever befalls you, remember that the King will always have one more move.

Chapter 4   Luke 5:33-39

Can Guests Fast?

We come to a question Jesus asked in view of some criticism He received from the religious people of the day. Let us look at the text surrounding it in Luke 5.

> They said to him, "John's disciples often fast and pray, and so do the disciples of the Pharisees, but yours go on eating and drinking." Jesus answered, "Can you make the guests of the bridegroom fast while he is with them? But the time will come when the bridegroom will be taken from them; in those days they will fast." [That is the metaphor] He told this parable: "No one tears a patch from a new garment and sews it on an old one. If he does, he will have torn the new garment, and the patch from the new will not match the old. And no one pours new wine into old wineskins. If he does, the new wine will burst the skins, the wine will run out and the wineskins will be ruined. No, new wine must be poured into new wineskins. And no one after drinking old wine wants the new, for he says, 'the old is better.'" Luke 5:33-39.

Note that Jesus answered the question He was asked by asking this question:

"Can you make the guests of the bridegroom fast while he is with them?" Luke 5:34.

The event recorded here is more than ancient history. This parable is the first of the 24 parables contained in Luke's Gospel. A parable is a profound teaching tool that Jesus utilised frequently. Our word "parable" is a transliteration of the actual Greek word, *parabolé*. The word comes from two words: *para*, meaning "alongside" and *bole*, meaning "to throw." A parable is where a speaker offers a story or a description and then "throws down alongside" the story a deeper meaning. In other words, parables are stories that contain additional truth below the surface. There is a parable in every miracle and a miracle in every parable. The "miracle" of a parable is that on the surface it appears to be a simple story but there are always several levels of truth associated with it. Whenever you study a parable of Jesus, it is much like peeling an onion. An onion has several layers. The outer peel is like the natural truth of the story but when you peel away that layer, there are other layers of truth to be found. For those readers who enjoy studying figures of speech, a parable is considered to be a short allegory.

Jesus is going to use a powerful metaphor in the form of a wedding celebration. Then he is going to offer two short parables. One is about a patch of cloth and the other is about wineskins. It is important to remember that God inspired the entire Bible. It is a miracle book because the truth contained in the Bible is timeless. What Jesus said applied to those people living centuries ago and it applies just as appropriately and powerfully to us. As we examine these three topics of Jesus here, I want to introduce each one of them with a personal question that Jesus answers. Then I want to peel away three layers of truth. They are the surface, spiritual and personal truths.

- FIRST, we will peel away the surface truth. This is the natural story of the metaphor or parable.
- SECOND, we will examine the spiritual truth below the surface. This layer applies to the people who were the immediate audience of Jesus.

We will find those two layers are fairly painless because they do not really apply to us. However, the THIRD is the layer of personal truth:

- It is the core of truth.
- It examines what God is saying to you and me.
- It is the most uncomfortable level.

Many preachers hesitate to venture onto this third level. It is dangerous preaching because personal truth often offends people. Religious people crucified Jesus because His truth offended them. When you peel an onion, you do not start crying until you get several layers down! We are going to consider:

THREE PERSONAL QUESTIONS

- Should I be sombre or joyful?
- Can I come to Christ and be the same?
- Do I have to accept new ideas?

1. SHOULD I BE SOMBRE OR JOYFUL?

Jesus' critics watched the way His disciples acted at Matthew's Salvation Party and they were offended. These religious snobs equated spirituality with suffering. The more pained the expressions on your face, the more holy that they assumed you were. This strange spiritual masochism still prevails today. Some religions require people to deface their bodies or walk on hot coals or sit on beds of needles. They associate pain with purity. I have read of scores of people who walk on bloodied knees for many miles just to pray in a certain church. So we ask the questions:

- Is this what Jesus taught?
- Is the correct spiritual disposition sombreness and suffering or joy and gladness?

The suffering Pharisees pointed out that they fasted and the disciples of John the Baptist fasted and both of these statements were true. In total contrast, Jesus' disciples partied. To say the Pharisees fasted is a grave understatement! They fasted two days each week but they were fasting for the wrong reason. They were doing it simply as an outward display of their self perceived righteousness. In other words, they were not fasting for God's sake; they were fasting to be seen by others. The Pharisees would fast from sunrise to sunset on Tuesdays and Thursdays, about twelve hours. They often put limestone dust or ashes on their faces and in their hair. They wore burlap or sackcloth and sucked their cheeks so as to appear gaunt and emaciated. That was their bizarre way of looking holy. They "fasted" to show off, so others could see how religious they were. Fasting itself is a wonderful spiritual discipline. Jesus often fasted and prayed but it was not a ritual designed for others to see.

When you examine the Old Testament, there is only *one* day a year when the Jewish Nation was commanded to fast and that was Yom Kippur, the Day of Atonement. But these Pharisees took a God given rule of spiritual discipline and changed it into a symbol of super-self-righteousness.

In answering their criticism, Jesus employed a powerful metaphor. Let us "peel the onion" to understand what Jesus was saying.

FIRST, the SURFACE TRUTH

A Jewish wedding is a scene of celebration.

I have discovered from studying Jewish literature there were three matters that distinguish the Eastern weddings from our Western weddings.

- First, the Eastern wedding was the culmination of a year of betrothal. That time of anticipation and planning was much more involved than the engagement period that is more common in the West.
- Second, there was a week of eating, dancing, singing and celebrating at the home of the groom's father following the wedding. In my country, couples leave immediately after the wedding reception for a honeymoon. After the reception, the celebrations are over for the family and friends.
- Third, in Jewish weddings, the groom and bride were treated like royalty, king and queen, even given garland crowns to wear during the weeklong celebration. It was the best week of their lives and the friends of the bridegroom did some serious partying. There was food, drink, dancing, music and fun for an entire week.

Let us peel off another layer of truth and go deeper.

SECOND, the SPIRITUAL TRUTH

They celebrated the presence of the Bridegroom

When the religious hypocrites challenged Jesus about His disciples' joyful behaviour, He made an amazing comparison. He claimed to be like a bridegroom and His disciples like the guests at a wedding celebration. That is why they were happy instead of being sombre. It was a time of celebration. A most important spiritual as well as a very practical point that we need to learn from this passage of Scripture, is that the Christian life should be more like a wedding celebration than a funeral service. Consider the real issue that the Pharisees were complaining about. Their complaint could be put like this:

"It is not fair for you people to enjoy life when we have to endure religion! If you were really holy, you would be miserable like us!" The Pharisees were:

- Griping while Jesus' disciples were grinning.
- Sombre, while Jesus' disciples were singing.
- Languishing while Jesus' disciples were laughing.
- Criticising while Jesus' disciples were celebrating.
- Jealous while Jesus' disciples were jubilant.

Which group do you associate yourself with? Let us peel off another layer of truth and go deeper.

THIRD, the PERSONAL TRUTH

Awareness of Jesus brings joy even during a fast

I have been observing Christians closely for many years and I have found that there are modern "Pharisees" in the church today. Some people seem to agree with the Pharisees that the more miserable you look in church, the more "holy" you must be. Have you met people who outside of the church building are likeable and tell jokes? But when they go inside they put on what I call the "Holy Look." Perhaps you have seen it. It is an expression somewhere between acid indigestion and a migraine headache. Many Christians have loosened up a lot in recent years but there are still plenty of folks in church who look as though they have been drinking pickle vinegar.

- Do you experience the "joy of the Lord" in your daily Christian life?
- If you once knew the "joy of the Lord", why has it gone?
- Why do you leave the "joy of the Lord" at home when you attend church?

❏ Where did the idea that laughter is unholy or unscriptural originate?

What does the Book of Proverbs teach us?

"A cheerful heart is good medicine, but a crushed spirit dries up the bones." Proverbs 17:22.

Some people say that you have got to be serious at all times and they seem to think that this teaching originates in the Bible. They are wrong. There are times to weep and there are times to laugh and a wise person knows the difference. But life does not cease to be serious when you laugh any more than it ceases to be funny when you cry. The Christian life is best characterised by joy. When you are aware of the presence of the Lord with you, you cannot help but rejoice, whatever you are doing and wherever you are. This is the way David described the source of our joy:

"You have made known to me the path of life; you will fill me with joy in your presence, with eternal pleasures at your right hand." Psalm 16:11.

In this parable, Jesus is commenting upon the joy that should characterise our lives when we discover the reality of a relationship with Him. Regrettably, church services have for far too many centuries mirrored an Old Testament concept of worship. This is the background:

❏ The Old Testament form of worship was based on a pattern or model that was specified by God in the Law of Moses and you can read the details of what had to happen during the various services in the Books of Leviticus and Deuteronomy.
❏ The rituals were part of The Commandments given by God to Moses. Because of this, they were not optional

or variable and consequently, each new generation of the Jewish Nation worshipped God in exactly the same way in identical services.
- ❏ Over hundreds of years, innumerable animals were sacrificed during these services. The reasons for this:
  - First, the worshippers were reminded that their sin deserved to be punished by death but that God in His love and mercy would accept the death of a substitute on their behalf.
  - Second, the sacrifice was a picture of what would one day happen at Calvary when the sinless Saviour would suffer and die on behalf of sinners.
- ❏ The New Testament does not teach that Christian services should be characterised by ritual and silence with everyone in awe- stricken solemnity.

Let me ask you this very important question.

Why has the death of Jesus made such an important and significant change in the way God is worshipped?

- ❏ We celebrate what Jesus has done for us on the Cross.
- ❏ We never forget the tremendous suffering that Jesus willingly endured for our sins but we rejoice in the Salvation that His death on our behalf has brought us.
- ❏ We know that because Jesus was raised from the dead, He defeated death and death has no power to stop believers being resurrected.

Those who behave like the Pharisees should realise that in 1Corinthians 15:19 Paul tells us that only unbelievers are entitled to be miserable.

The following represent the picture of the Christian life

that Jesus came to give:

- Instead of the fast, it is a feast.
- Instead of the sackcloth, there is a robe.
- Instead of solemnity, there ought to be joy.

One reason why the church is written off by people who come to see if Christianity is for them is the deathly dullness of what some Christians call worship. The joy that should characterise our lives when we discover the reality of a relationship with Jesus Christ does not mean that we will not encounter illness or suffering. Sure, there will be sadness, pain and disappointment this side of Heaven. If you compare the Christian life to a song, the melody line is always joy and praise. The harmony line at times will be suffering and pain. When we add the melody and the harmony together, our lives are a beautiful song but the melody of joy and praise must prevail. Jesus addressed this. He said:

"In this world you shall have trouble—but take heart! For I have overcome the world!" John 16:33.

Do not misunderstand what Jesus was saying to the religious people who criticised His disciples for the joyful way they were behaving. Jesus did not condemn fasting. In verse 35 Jesus used fasting only as an illustration when He was predicting His death. He spoke of the time:

"when the bridegroom will be taken from them; in those days they will fast." Luke 5:35

The word "taken" means to be "ripped away violently." Jesus was saying that only after His brutal death would His followers fast. But they would never fast like the Pharisees fasted. They would never whiten their faces, pile ashes on their hair and moan and groan so that everyone would know how "spiritual" they were. During His "Sermon on the Mount", Jesus gave these instructions about fasting to His disciples:

"When you fast, do not look sombre as the hypocrites do, for they disfigure their faces to show men they are fasting . . . when you fast, put oil on you head and wash your face, so that it will not be obvious to men that you are fasting, but only to your Father..." Matthew 6:16.

As we conclude our consideration of the first part of the parable, three questions must be asked.

- Are we like the Pharisees or the disciples of Jesus?
- Is there real joy in our life?
- If someone closely observed our life for a month would they say, "I want what they have?"

2. CAN I COME TO CHRIST AND BE THE SAME?

The beautiful thing about Jesus' use of parables is that He used simple everyday tasks and ideas to communicate deep spiritual truth. He talked about sewing a new piece of cloth onto an old garment. Let us take only a brief moment to "peel the onion" starting at the surface truth.

FIRST, the SURFACE TRUTH

New cloth sewn on old cloth will rip the old

Today we have developed all kinds of synthetic fabrics that do not shrink when washed. In Jesus' time, new cloth would always shrink after the first few washes. A person wearing a new garment had to make sure it was couple of sizes too large so that over time, the garment would shrink down to the right size. Garments were often torn or moth eaten so they were constantly repaired. If you had an old robe with a hole in it, it would be foolish to sew a new patch of cloth on it. Obviously, when it was washed, the new patch would shrink but the old cloth would stay the same. That was just common good sense back then. It would have ruined both the new patch and the old garment.

Now let us look a layer deeper.

SECOND, the SPIRITUAL TRUTH.

Jesus did not come to "patch up" the Old Covenant

Jesus' immediate audience knew what He was talking about. The old garment was the Old Testament, or the Old Covenant, what we would call "The Law."

- Jesus said He had not come to improve the Old Covenant.
- Jesus came to replace the Old Covenant with something totally new.

There was no way His new covenant could be used to "patch up" the old one. The new Age of Grace had dawned.

John said it well when he wrote:

"The law was given through Moses [that is the old]; grace and truth [that is the new] came through Jesus Christ." John 1:17.

Jesus came to institute an entire new system of faith and His enemies did not like it.

Let us peel off another layer and go deeper.

THIRD, the PERSONAL TRUTH

Jesus creates us totally anew

Some people think that they are pretty good and only need Jesus to come and "patch up" their lives. I heard the story of a mother who had many children. One of her boys fell down on a new laid road and was covered in tar. He was a mess. His mother was outside trying to clean the sticky tar off of him. She said, "You know Tom, it would be easier to just have another one than to clean you up!"

That is what happens to us. Jesus does not try to clean our old hearts. He gives us a new heart. When Jesus comes into your life, His goal is not to reform you. He will transform you. We are all sinners by nature and by choice. That is why to try to "fix" our sinful character is like sewing a new un-shrunk patch on an old garment. Sooner or later we would hear the Rrrrriiiiipp! At the time of our PHYSICAL birth we were deformed by sin.

That is why Jesus says we need a new SPIRITUAL birth. 2 Corinthians says:

"Therefore if anyone is in Christ, he is a new creation; the old has gone, the new has come!" 2 Corinthians. 5:17.

Jesus deepened the parable about old and new by talking about wine in wineskins. Here is the point He addresses.

3. DO I HAVE TO ACCEPT NEW IDEAS?

Let us remove different layers of meaning in this parable.

FIRST, the SURFACE TRUTH

New wine in old wineskins will burst them.

We use casks and bottles to hold wine today but in Jesus' time, wine was stored in goatskins. These skins were removed, scraped clean on the inside and then tanned over a fire. Then the skin was stitched back together with the neck of the goatskin becoming the neck of the wineskin. A new wineskin was soft and supple. When new wine was poured into it, gas was released from the process of fermentation and the new wineskin would stretch to accommodate the expansion.

Jesus often employed subtle humour in His teaching. At that time, anything that was silly or foolish was comical, like straining out a gnat and swallowing a camel. This parable is funny because Jesus is insinuating that only a fool would put new wine in an old wineskin. Everyone listening probably rolled about with laughter because they knew what would happen. An old wineskin had already expanded and hardened from previous wine. It stopped expanding and became hardened. It was hilarious to imagine the result of pouring new wine into an old wineskin. Over a period of just a few days there would be audible sounds as the hard skin began to crack and split. The gas was expanding but the old skin was too inflexible to change its shape. The old skin could not stretch and soon the stitches would start to blow. You can almost hear the old wineskin stretching and straining until "pop!" the seams burst open and the new wine is lost.

What do you think Jesus is implying?

Let us go a little deeper.

SECOND, the SPIRITUAL TRUTH

We must not lose the ability to change

The religious leaders of Jesus' day did not like His teaching because it was new. He said things that they had never heard before. His new teaching shocked and offended them. He did things that they had never seen done before. They were appalled that He ate and drank with sinners! The religious leaders could not handle this "new wine" that Jesus was offering. They were like inflexible old wineskins. Their attitude was "If it is new, it cannot be true!" Every time Jesus said or did something new you could almost hear the sound of straining and stretching until "pop!" they killed the Messenger instead of accepting His message.

If we stop learning or being open to new truth, we place ourselves in a hazardous spiritual condition. We must never lose the ability to have our minds stretched. Jesus Himself recognised that it is much more comfortable and pleasant to stick with the "old ways." That is why He said:

"no one after drinking the old wine wants the new, for he says, 'the old is better.'" Luke 5:39.

Do not misunderstand what Jesus said. He was not making a judgement about the superiority of aged wine. He was making an observation about our human nature. We like changing our old cars for new cars and changing our houses for bigger ones but we do not spiritual change. We do not like new ways, new ideas or new truth. Nobody enjoys change. We all enjoy our normal "routines." We like to sit in the same seat at church every Sunday. All routines become habits and habits become ruts. We fail to realise that a rut is nothing but a grave with both ends kicked out.

Human nature rebels against anything that seems to threaten the "good old days" and the "good old ways." The truth of this parable is clear:

- ❏ Jesus is the New Patch.
- ❏ Jesus is the New Wine.

Consider this. God loves new things:

- ❏ We enter the Christian life through a new birth.
- ❏ We become a new creation.
- ❏ We walk in newness of life.
- ❏ We read the New Testament.

And one day God will create a New Heaven and a New Earth. One of the last things that Jesus states in the Bible:

> "I am making everything new." Revelation 21:5.

Whilst God delights in making new things, our motto is that "If it's not broken, don't fix it". Jesus compared that attitude to an old wineskin and He actually said that if you do not fix it, you will break!

This attitude of resisting new truth is nothing new. It was present during Jesus' time and it has always characterised human history:

- ❏ When Galileo invented a crude telescope and began to study the stars, he dared to introduce the radical new idea that perhaps the Earth was not the centre of the universe. In fact, he was so brazen as to suggest that the Earth actually rotated around the Sun rather than the Sun circling the earth. "Heresy!" said the Established Church. It was like pouring new wine into old wineskins. In 1633 he was put on trial as a heretic.

He was found guilty and placed under permanent house arrest. Why could not the leaders of the Inquisition accept this "new idea?" Was it for the reason that Jesus gave, "the old wine is better"? They were old wineskins. They could not accept new wine.

- The Modern Missions movement was not launched until 200 years ago. At the time, the idea of sending Christian missionaries to other countries was radical. When a young English shoemaker, William Carey, studied the maps of the travels of Captain Cook, he became burdened for the millions of people in these lands who did not know Christ. So, he became a minister and studied foreign languages. He went to a religious convention and dared to stand up and asked whether the Great Commission obliged them to take the Gospel to foreign nations. An older minister rebuked him and asked him to sit down saying that when it pleased God to covert the heathen, He would do it without aid from either of them. It was like pouring new wine into old wineskins. But William Carey travelled to India to preach the Gospel and he became the father of Modern Missions.

Let us think about you and me. Let us peel off another layer and go deeper.

THIRD, the PERSONAL TRUTH

We must be aware that inflexibility and hardness of heart will cause difficulty and pain in our lives

Jesus was addressing an attitude that resists change or anything new. This was the attitude of the religious leaders that challenged Jesus and one we need to guard against. Like an old hardened wineskin, our hearts and minds can calcify until they become so inflexible that we cannot accept any change. When "new wine" is introduced to us, we crack and split and make a mess. The Bible issues a warning to us about the danger of a hardened heart:

"Today, if you hear his voice, do not harden your hearts as you did in the rebellion" Hebrews 3:15.

The children of Israel refused to go into the Promised Land. They became lazy because God fed them manna and they did not have to fight any battles. When faced with the new idea of going into Canaan and taking the land by force they said that they "liked the old wine better." And God said: *"Okay, you are going to take another lap around Mount Sinai . . . and another . . . and another."* For forty years they wandered in the old paths, eating the same old manna. Why? They refused to accept the "new wine of God's plan" for their future. What kind of person are we?

- Are we like an old wineskin?
- Have we become moulded into a certain mental state or emotional disposition?
- Are we not going to change for anything?
- Can others anticipate what our attitude will be when any new idea or concept is about to be discussed or introduced? It may be a new building programme, a new schedule, a new method or indeed anything. It really is sad if others can anticipate that we will not listen to any new proposals. Can they almost hear us straining, and cracking, until 'pop!' we blow a stitch and express our anger and opposition?

Whether we like it or not, this parable teaches the dangers of us being "inflexible old wineskins". A church minister told me several years ago, that when he suggested that everyone dress casually in church during the summer months, you would have thought that he had changed the words in John 3:16! It was a new idea. Some people still do not think you can worship unless you are dressed in your very best clothes.

Even if you do not consider yourself as one who opposes every new suggestion, or inhibits all changes, in reality, how flexible are you? What about moving the time of the Sunday services, different worship styles, a variety of music, different methods . . . the list goes on and on?

I like the extra Beatitude that says, "Blessed are the flexible for they shall not be bent out of shape."

Let us consider the reality of the situation in another context. Would you go to a doctor who only practised the medicine and procedures used:

- Forty years ago?
- One hundred and forty years ago?
- Over two hundred years ago?

I think I can accurately guess your answer. You see, when we put our "resistance to change" attitude to the test, we tend to find that we are selective and are happy to change so many things in our lives except spiritual matters.

The amazing thing to remember about old wineskins is that at one time they were new wineskins and they were flexible enough to expand. As you get older it becomes harder and harder to accept new spiritual ideas and methods. It is as if the mind loses the ability to stretch. We get to the point where we suspect everything that is new and different. This is exactly what Jesus was warning against.

We need to be open to:

- New ideas.
- New methods.
- New revelations of truth.

Let me explain. God has already revealed all He wishes His people to know so in reality, there is no new truth for God to reveal to us today. But unless we know all the truth that God has revealed, we must always be a willing to learn and accept new revelations of the truth to us.

Sadly, we like the old wine, the old ways. Do we really expect God to bless us and our service? We must heed the parable and guard ourselves against becoming like old hard wineskins.

Rudyard Kipling once accompanied General William Booth, founder of the Salvation Army, to a foreign country. They were met by a group of Christians who were dancing and playing tambourines. Kipling, a proper young Englishman, was shocked by this activity. His orthodox soul resented the dancing and the tambourines and he expressed his displeasure to General Booth. Booth told the young man that if he thought he could win one more soul for Christ by standing on his head and beating a tambourine with his feet, he would learn how to do it.

We have been considering parties, patches, and wineskins. They are the subjects that raise questions for us to answer as we conclude this chapter:

- Do we need to stop behaving as though the Christian life is a funeral service and start celebrating the truth that we belong to a Bridegroom who is coming back soon for us?
- Do we need to stop trying to patch up our old lives and allow Jesus to put a new robe of righteousness on us?

- Jesus is providing plenty of the new wine for us but:

  - Have we stopped growing?
  - Have we stopped changing?
  - Have we become like an old, crusty, wineskin?

When some six year olds were being taught the story of Solomon's wisdom, the children were asked to think about what they might ask God to give them if they could ask for whatever they wanted. One little girl's eyes just went into a trance as she excitedly pondered the question. Then she looked at the teacher with a little bewilderment in those eyes and said *"I don't even know what He's got up there"*. How much truth is contained in the wisdom of a child! As I think about it, I realise that sometimes I am hesitant to ask God for anything specific for the same reason. I am aware that God can do so much more than I ask or think. How do I even begin to know what to ask for? My concern is that I ask for something inferior when God has something so much better that He wants to give me:

- I ask for health. God offers His strength.
- I ask for financial assistance. God offers His riches.
- I ask for loved ones to live a few days longer. God offers eternal life.
- I ask for physical well-being, peace and comfort. God offers His very presence.

So much of what I ask for is so petty compared to all that God has at His disposal and I guess you think the same. That little girl was right. We do not know all He has for us. That is why we must not be content with mere religion when we can have new experiences of Christ's presence in us that will enable Him to do new things through us. Look at the alternatives available and make your choices:

- Grim religion rather than grace religion.
- Liturgy without life.
- The mundane when we can have the momentous.

Reflect on what the Apostle Paul prayed for the Ephesians:

"I keep asking that the God of our Lord Jesus Christ, the glorious Father, may give you the Spirit of wisdom and revelation so that you may know him better. I pray also that the eyes of your heart may be enlightened in order that you may know the hope to which he has called you, the riches of his glorious inheritance in the saints, and his incomparably great power for us who believe." Ephesians 1:17-18.

Let us settle for nothing less.

Chapter 5   1 Kings 19

What Are You Doing Here?

The story is told of ten-year-old Johnny, who rushes home from school one day. He invades the fridge and is scooping out some cherry vanilla ice cream when his mother enters the kitchen. She says, "Put that away, Johnny. You cannot have ice cream now. It is too close to suppertime. Go outside and play." Johnny whimpers and says, "There is no one to play with." Trying to pacify him, she says, "OK. I will play with you. What do you want to play?" He says, "I want to play Mums and Dad." To appease him, she says, "Fine, I will play. What do I do?" Johnny says, "You go in the living room and sit down." Mum goes into the living room. Johnny, feeling a bit bold, swaggers down the hall and opens the utility door. He dons his father's old fishing hat and overcoat. He goes into the living room, sits down, picks up the remote and starts changing TV channels. His mother says, "What do I do now?" In a gruff manner, Johnny says, "Go in the kitchen and get that kid some ice cream!"

What a child would give to be a mum or dad for a day. I hesitate to think what would be the result. But, suppose you could be God for a while. Ever played the game, "If I were God..." If I were God, I suspect I would be tempted to be a bit like Johnny. "Get that boy some money! Whatever he wants, you make sure he gets it! And take away those problems that make life difficult for him!"

Since that is what we think we would do, we do not understand it when God does not act that way. But like a ten-year-old who does not understand the wisdom of his parents, we seldom understand the wisdom of an Almighty God. That is the point of the Book of Job. Chapter after chapter Job said: *"God, I do not understand why these things are happening!"* God's response is, *"You do not need to know why; you just need to know Me."* The Psalmist put it like this:

"I will exalt you, my God the King; I will praise your name for ever and ever. Every day I will praise you, and I will extol your name for ever and ever. Great is the LORD and most worthy of praise; his greatness no-one can fathom." Psalm 145:1-2.

1 Kings 19 reveals a question that an angel asked Elijah, a great prophet of God, when Elijah was very discouraged. *"What are you doing here Elijah?"* Let us look at the text surrounding it in 1 Kings 19.

Now Ahab told Jezebel everything Elijah had done and how he had killed all the prophets with the sword. So Jezebel sent a messenger to Elijah to say, "May the gods deal with me, be it ever so severely, if by this time tomorrow I do not make your life like that of one of them." Elijah was afraid and ran for his life. When he came to Beersheba in Judah, he left his servant there, while he himself went a day's journey into the desert. He came to a broom tree, sat down under it and prayed that he might die. "I have had enough, LORD," he said. "Take my life; I am no better than my ancestors." Then he lay down under the tree and fell asleep. All at once an angel touched him and said, "Get up and eat." He looked around, and there by his head was a cake of bread baked over hot coals, and a jar of water. He ate and drank and then lay down again. The angel of the LORD came back a second time and touched him and said, "Get up and eat, for the journey is too much for you." So he got up and ate and drank. Strengthened by that food, he travelled forty days and forty nights until he reached Horeb, the mountain of God. There he went into a cave and spent the night. And the word of the LORD came to him: "What are you doing here, Elijah?" He replied, "I have been very zealous for the LORD God Almighty. The Israelites have rejected your covenant, broken down your altars, and put your prophets to death with the sword. I am the only one left, and now they are trying to kill me too." The LORD said, "Go out and stand on the mountain in the presence of the LORD, for the LORD is about to pass by." Then a great and powerful wind tore the mountains apart and shattered the rocks before the LORD, but the LORD was not in the wind. After the wind there was an earthquake, but the LORD was not in the earthquake. After the earthquake came a fire, but the LORD was not in the fire. And after the fire came a gentle whisper. When Elijah heard it, he pulled his cloak over his face and went out and stood at the mouth of the cave. Then a voice said to him, "What are you doing here, Elijah?" He replied, "I have been very zealous for the LORD God Almighty. The Israelites have rejected your covenant, broken down your altars, and put your prophets to death with the sword. I am the only one left, and now they are trying to kill me too." The LORD said to him, "Go back the way you came, and go to the Desert of Damascus. When you get there, anoint Hazael king over Aram. Also, anoint Jehu son of Nimshi king over Israel, and anoint Elisha son of Shaphat from Abel Meholah to succeed you as prophet. Jehu will put to death any who escape the sword of Hazael, and Elisha will put to death any who escape the sword of Jehu. Yet I reserve seven thousand in Israel—all whose knees have not bowed down to Baal and all whose mouths have not kissed him." So Elijah went from there and found Elisha son of Shaphat. He was ploughing with twelve yoke of oxen, and he himself was driving the twelfth pair. Elijah went up to him and threw his cloak around him. Elisha then left his oxen and ran after Elijah. "Let me kiss my father and mother good-by," he said, "and then I will come with you." "Go back," Elijah replied. "What have I done to you?" So Elisha left him and went back. He took his yoke of oxen and slaughtered them. He burned the ploughing equipment to cook the meat and gave it to the people, and they ate. Then he set out to follow Elijah and became his attendant. 1 Kings 19.

We do live in strange times. Someone has called this the *Age of Anxiety,* and it seems appropriate enough. I do not blame anyone for feeling a bit shaky as we think about what is happening today in our world. Patience is in short supply everywhere. I ran across a little poem that seems to describe contemporary life:

This is the age of the half-read page
And the quick bash, and the mad dash
The bright night, with the nerves tight
The plane hop, with a brief stop
The lamp tan in a short span
The big shot in a good spot
And the brain strain and the heart pain
And the cat-naps, till the spring snaps
And the fun's done!

We are meeting Elijah when he is in trouble. He is

depressed, discouraged, stressed, burned out, mentally strained, physically drained and spiritually out of sorts. He is exactly like most of us! The next to the last line of that poem seems to perfectly describe Elijah when it speaks of the *brain strain and the heart pain*. At some point, if you keep on pushing, "the spring snaps and the fun's done". For Elijah, the fun was done, at least for a while. Our text describes how God met him at his lowest point.

A leading Christian psychiatrist was being interviewed on TV discussing the physical and medical factors that can lead to depression. He remarked that for most Christians, depression is basically a spiritual issue. My experience confirms that this view is correct because the depression suffered by some Christians could be a symptom of underlying spiritual issues that need to be faced and addressed. Of course, it is necessary to use all medical means that are appropriate to treat depression. There could well be genuine medical issues involved but it would be foolish to ignore any spiritual problems that might be causing the depression.

Certainly Elijah was depressed and discouraged. After his great victory on Mount Carmel, where he had defied idol worshippers and won the day, I think he expected the Nation of Israel to experience a vast turning to the Lord. But when Queen Jezebel threatened him, he cracked under the pressure and ran south to Beersheba and from Beersheba he went a day's journey into the desert. There he sat under a broom tree in utter dejection. Judging himself a failure, he prays that God might take his life.

His predicament is common to us all. What greater minds like Elijah's have felt intensely, we all have felt in our own degree. Many of us have felt our hearts aching for want of sympathy. We have had our lonely hours, our days of disappointment, our moments of hopelessness and times when our highest feelings have been misunderstood and our purest feelings met with ridicule. We have known days when our heavy secret was lying unshared, like ice upon the heart. And then the spirit gives way. Because we are all made of the same clay, let us pay close attention to how God deals with His discouraged servant Elijah. We read that he needed four things and those he received from God. Elijah needed:

- Rest and Refreshment.
- To Face His Fears.
- A New Vision of God.
- A New Commission.

ONE: Elijah Needed Rest and Refreshment

Elijah sat under the broom tree so discouraged that he prayed that he might die. Then he fell asleep. The Lord sent an angel with a command from Heaven:

> "All at once an angel touched him and said, "Get up and eat'."
> 1Kings 19:5.

What about that for spiritual advice? The angel did not say, "Get up and pray", "Get up and read the Word", "Get up and start preaching", or "Get up and serve the Lord". An angel came from Heaven to tell Elijah he needed to eat. Is this advice such a profound truth? Yes. We are human beings and we need to eat. We also need to sleep. Maybe at time we need to eat and sleep even more than we need to pray. There is a time for everything. There is a time for crying out to God and there is a time to roll over in bed, close your eyes and get a good sleep. Sometimes we might need to let our hair down and have a blast. For some that means going for a short walk. For others it means hiking in the mountains. For some it means sitting in a comfortable chair and knitting. For me it means reading. We were not made to work every day without rest:

- From the creation story we know that God built into the fabric of the Universe that the seventh day was a special day of rest.
- The Law of Moses required the Sabbath day to be a day of rest.
- The Israelites could only work for six days a week under penalty of death for disobedience.

We need to work and to work hard and serve the Lord but we also need a time of rest and relaxation. Sometimes we need to follow the spiritual and sensible advice of the angel to get up and have a good meal. Why? Because you will feel so much better. Elijah looked around and found a cake of bread baked over hot coals and a jar of water. He ate and drank and then he lay down and slept again. God's mountain man is tuckered out. He took a nap. He got up, had some food and he went back to bed again. Is he lazy? No. He is just worn out in the service of God. So:

"The angel of the LORD came back a second time and touched him and said, "Get up and eat, for the journey is too much for you." 1Kings 19:7.

Strengthened by that food he travelled forty days and forty nights until he reached Horeb, the Mountain of God. There he went into a cave and spent the night there. Understand that he still has all kind of problems. We have not got to the real issues of life yet. Sometimes you cannot get to the deep issues until you deal with things like hunger and exhaustion. Basically God arranged for Elijah to have a six-week vacation, all expenses paid. That sounds good until you recall that he had to walk across the desert by himself to Mount Sinai.

Why did he go to Horeb? Because he knew Mount Sinai was the place you went to when you knew you needed to meet God. He did not just pick any mountain. If he wanted to find a cave, there were caves a lot closer than Horeb. He went back to where Moses met God. There is a value in going back to certain milestones in your life where you met God in the past. When you are depressed, there are at least three things you need and God made sure Elijah got all three of them:

- You need good food.
- You need rest.
- You need some physical exercise.

I would consider walking forty days across the desert more than enough physical exercise. I am sure you would too! Whilst we need more than food, rest and exercise we must realise that these are an essential start on the road to both physical and spiritual recovery. But there is more to come.

TWO: Elijah Needed to Face His Fears

"And the word of the Lord came to him: 'What are you doing here...?'" 1Kings:19:9.

That is a great question. The last time we saw Elijah, he was winning a great victory for God on Mount Carmel. So what is he doing cowering in a cave, hundreds of miles away? Not that the Lord did not know. This question was not for God's benefit but for Elijah's. "Explain yourself, Elijah. You were my prophet on Mount Carmel. What are you doing here?" God is saying to Elijah that it was time to face his fears. This is Elijah's response:

"I have been very zealous for the LORD God Almighty. The Israelites have rejected your covenant, broken down your altars, and put your prophets to death with the sword." 1Kings:19:14.

Everything Elijah said was true.

- ❏ He has been zealous.
- ❏ The people had rejected God's covenant.
- ❏ The people had put prophets to death.

No exaggeration at all. If he had stopped there, he would have been on solid ground. Read what he said next:

"I am the only one left, and now they are trying to kill me too." 1Kings:19:14.

The last part of Elijah response was true, his life was in danger. The first part was not true because he was not the only one left. But it was that feeling of being utterly alone that needed an adjustment. He had sunk so deep in self-pity that he actually thought he was the only righteous man left in Israel. Let me at this point make a simple application:

SELF-PITY IS THE ENEMY OF SPIRITUAL GROWTH

As long as we feel sorry for ourselves, we will make excuses for not facing our own problems and we will never get better. I know of a man who got in trouble because of his misuse of the Internet. He got drawn into pornography and ended up committing adultery. It nearly cost him his marriage. He said that part of his restoration process included going to a weekly meeting of men struggling with all sorts of sexual sins. It was a very tough group. They had one rule and only one. NO SELF-PITY. They would not let you blame your:

- Wife.
- Colleagues.
- Parents.
- Inner tendencies.
- Childhood experiences.

If you started down the "road of self–pity" they would stop you. And he said that if you continued, they threw you out of the group. The group recognised the dangers of self-pity to their restoration process. I repeat:

SELF-PITY IS THE ENEMY OF SPIRITUAL GROWTH

That statement may be the most important thing I have to pass on. We must face our problems and make the adjustments that are needed. As long as we:

- Feel sorry for ourselves: we will never get better.
- Blame others: we will never get better.
- Offload our problems onto somebody else: we will never get better.
- Say, "Lord, I am the only faithful one left": we will never get better.

Do some of you reading these words have spiritual problems because:

- You are wallowing in self-pity?
- You have convinced yourself that other people cause your problems?
- You blame your circumstances for your problems?

You need no longer wonder why you are you not getting better and your problems continue. You are stuck and you will remain stuck until you stop making excuses and start taking responsibility for your problems. You cannot and you will not get better because: SELF-PITY IS THE MORTAL ENEMY OF ALL SPIRITUAL GROWTH.

THREE: Elijah Needed a New Vision of God

Note how these three things go together for Elijah. He needed to be changed body, mind and soul:

- Rest and relaxation speaks to his body.
- Facing his fears and self-pity speaks to his mind.
- A new vision of God speaks to the need of his soul.

When Elijah began to wallow in self-pity, notice how God responded. Or more particularly,

NOTICE WHAT GOD DID NOT DO.

- Say what many of us would have said: "What is wrong with you? Get your act together. Come on. Snap out of it. Get a grip!"
- Argue with Elijah, as many of us would have done.
- Put Elijah down, rebuke or ridicule him.

NOTICE WHAT GOD DID:

God met Elijah at the point of his deep despair. God said:

"Go out and stand on the mountain in the presence of the LORD, for the LORD is about to pass by." 1Kings 19:11.

That is all God does. He does not condemn Elijah. If somebody condemns us when we are depressed it does not assist us and it does not assist when we condemn others. It just makes the situation worse. What follows is amazing. A mighty wind tore across the face of the mountain, shattering the rocks and we read:

- But the Lord was not in the wind. After the wind came an earthquake.
- But the Lord was not in the earthquake. After the earthquake came a fire.
- But the Lord was not in the fire. And after the fire came a gentle whisper and when Elijah heard it, he pulled his cloak over his face and he went out and stood in the mouth of the cave.

Some spirits must go through a discipline analogous to that experienced by Elijah. The storm-struggle must precede the still small voice. There are:

- Minds that must be convulsed with doubt before they can repose in faith.
- Hearts that must be broken with regret before they can rise into hope.
- Personalities which must have all things taken from them before they can find all things again in God.

When the tempest has spent its fury, we will be blessed if like Elijah, we listen for our Heavenly Father's voice and acknowledge His presence. Why did God put Elijah through this demonstration of divine power?

God wanted Elijah back in touch with spiritual reality. Psalm 46 says:

> "Be still and know that I am God." Psalm 46:10.

The Lord wants Elijah to know that it is not in the earthquakes or the fires or the huge events where we most often encounter Him.

We often meet God in the small, forgotten places of life. One of our problems is that we want to see:
- The earthquakes.
- The fires.
- The big demonstrations.
- The spectacular answers to prayer.

Be sure of this. God speaks loud enough for the willing ear to hear. I have found myself praying over and over: *"O Lord, open the eyes of my heart that I might see you everywhere."* It has enabled me to see God at work in places where I never saw Him before.

FOUR: Elijah Needed a New Commission

God repeated His question and Elijah repeated his answer. God decided that the time had come to correct Elijah's inaccurate information. So God gave Elijah the information that he needed. God said to him:

"Go back the way you came and go to the desert of Damascus." 1Kings 19:15.

It is a long journey from the Sinai desert, through the Holy Land, to the desert around Damascus. Then God gave Elijah some very specific instructions:

"When you get there, anoint Hazael king over Aram. Also, anoint Jehu son of Nimshi king over Israel and anoint Elisha son of Shaphat from Abel Meholah to succeed you as prophet. Jehu will put to death any who escape the sword of Hazael and Elisha will put to death any who escape the sword of Jehu. Yet I reserve seven thousand in Israel—all whose knees have not bowed down to Baal and all whose mouths have not kissed him." I Kings 19:15-18.

Elijah was not alone. Not only is God with him, God has 7000 in Israel who have not bowed down to Baal. Understand this. There is no spot in this world where God is not already there. God is not just to be seen in the big things of life. He is also to be seen in the stillness and in the small things. God is not limited by our small vision. In all of this God was saying to Elijah:

- You are not alone, I am with you.
- I have 7,000 more just like you.
- I am going to give you a man to be your protégée, partner and successor.
- You never were alone, you are not alone now and you are not going to be alone in the future.

Elijah had accomplished more than he ever thought or imagined. The 7000 were men and women who took strength from his brave confrontation with the prophets of Baal. So, contrary to what Elijah thought, his life for God had not been wasted after all. What lessons can we learn from this?

The FIRST LESSON: No life is wasted that is spent in the service of our Lord

This is the irony of the story. Out of Elijah's perceived failure came the assurance of his ultimate victory. He had touched the lives of thousands of people who, like him, would not bow down to Baal.

The SECOND LESSON: We are not in a position to estimate our own effectiveness

How can we judge whether our work for God has been successful or unsuccessful? You and I are as likely as Elijah to get it wrong. Only God can render the final verdict. We must do our best and leave the results with God. He knows the lives that have been changed by our service. We must never give Satan the opportunity to attack and dishearten us and he certainly will if we entertain doubts about our own usefulness to God.

The THIRD LESSON: Elijah's victory and his defeat come back to back

It is not a sin to be discouraged or depressed. It is what we do when we are discouraged and depressed or feeling hopeless and useless that matters. Experience has proved that some Christians feel guilt and are ashamed at times like these, because they incorrectly associate these problems with sin. Often they keep the problems to themselves and suffer the consequences of not seeking spiritual help at an early stage. Remember that Satan will be keen to attack us when we put ourselves in a vulnerable spiritual condition because we make his work of destroying our usefulness for God so much easier.

It is true that you must face your problems honestly because they are your sole responsibility but you must get all the help you need to do this from Christians who will support you.

AND ALWAYS REMEMBER THIS:

God is always with you. There is no pit so deep that the love of God is not deeper still. If you are discouraged, the Lord loves you. He will never forget you. Let these thoughts fill your mind and be your continual encouragement in your service for God.

Chapter 6   Matthew 18:21

How Many Times Shall I Forgive?

Teachers will tell you that asking questions can be a very effective teaching tool. In the process of seeking the answer to one question, skilled teachers can assist their students to think of other questions. These question and answer sessions enable students to learn more and increase their understanding.

The question we are considering in this chapter is crucial for both our spiritual and our physical well-being. In Matthew 18 Peter came to Jesus and asked:

"Lord how many times shall I forgive my brother when he sins against me? Up to seven times?" Matthew 18:21.

Peter asks his Teacher a question about forgiveness, an issue that we all have to deal with in life. In order to fully grasp the matter that Peter raises and to understand the truth concerning forgiveness, we must first ask:

- WHAT is forgiveness?
- WHY does God ask us to do something that is so hard to do?
- HOW can we forgive?

QUESTION 1: WHAT is Forgiveness?

Understanding forgiveness can be very difficult for us. In our culture genuine forgiveness is unusual. It is more common to be unforgiving than forgiving. Experience teaches us that it is a "dog-eat-dog" world that we live in, not a "dog-forgive-dog" world.

In his book *What's So Amazing About Grace,* Philip Yancey writes that un-forgiveness: "plays like a background static of life for families, nations, and institutions. Un-forgiveness is sadly our natural human state. We nurse sores, go to elaborate lengths to rationalise our behaviour, perpetuate family feuds, punish ourselves, punish others, all to avoid the most unnatural act of forgiving."

Yancey is right. In our society, real forgiveness is as rare as hen's teeth. Now, people may say they forgive. They say that they "bury the hatchet" but it seems as though they always keep a "map" that carefully marks the spot where they buried it so that they can dig it up when they need it. We say we forgive but what we really do is put our resentment in cold storage so that we can thaw it out when we need it. Let us be realistic. We "nurse" our grudges as if they were our precious children! Because we keep resentments and grudges where we can easily get to them, we demonstrate the opposite of forgiveness because to "forgive" literally means, *"to release or send away, to let off."* Forgiving is a commitment not to let feelings of resentment come between us and the wrongdoer.

Forgiveness is built around the root word, "give" which should tell us that it is something that is given even though it is undeserved. There is a great deal of grace in the act of forgiveness. Forgiveness is not the norm. Perhaps the best way to answer this first question and to truly understand what forgiveness is and involves, is to remind ourselves of what it is not. Forgiveness is not:

- Forgetting
- Reconciliation
- Condonation
- Pardon.

FORGIVENESS is not FORGETTING

When people hurt us, we cannot simply forget what they have done and wipe it from our minds. We do not have that ability! No, determining to forgive someone means that every time the wrong comes to mind, we forgive them again. Colossians 3:13 literally says "Keep on forgiving one another." So forgiveness is a continuous process. I think this is what Jesus meant when He told Peter that we are to forgive one another not seven times but seventy times seven. Jesus was trying to get His student to understand that forgiving is something we do over and over and over again. It is not forgetting. In fact, it actually has more to do with remembering!

Clara Barton, the founder of the American Red Cross, was once reminded of something mean that someone had done to her years before. But she acted as if she had never even heard of the incident. "Do not you remember it?" her friend asked. "No," she said, "In fact I distinctly remember forgetting it."

FORGIVENESS is not RECONCILIATION

Forgiveness does not require the consent of the person who is being forgiven. We can forgive someone even if they do not ask or want to be forgiven. Reconciliation on the other hand would require their consent.

FORGIVENESS is not CONDONATION

Forgiveness does not require us to change our own views as to right and wrong or lower our own standards. We do not need to pretend that what has been done is not wrong, nor do we need to find excuses for the offender. No. Forgiveness involves taking the offence against us seriously. Forgiveness acknowledges the act as being wrong and forgives it anyway.

FORGIVENESS is not PARDON

A pardon is a legal process by which an offender is released from the consequences of a conviction, such as imprisonment. You can forgive and still insist on a just punishment for the offence committed against you.

In the home a parent might say to a teenager, "I forgive you for going to that party you had been forbidden from attending but you are still grounded." We might say to a friend who has gossiped or slandered us, "I forgive you for talking about me behind my back but it is going to be a while before I can give you my trust again."

Another thing, FORGIVENESS is not EASY

It can be extremely difficult to forgive. Perhaps this is one side affect of our sinful state. Forgiving seems to go against our grain. It is so much easier for us to SEEK revenge than to GIVE forgiveness. Despite listening to many sermons on forgiveness, we do not forgive easily, nor find ourselves easily forgiven. Forgiveness, we discover, is always harder than the sermons make it out to be. We have to work at it. We have to be realistic and honest with ourselves and accept that forgiveness does not come easily to us. We have dealt with the first question but our answer brings the second question to my mind.

QUESTION 2: WHY would God ask us to do something that is so hard to do?

There are four reasons why forgiving others will be well

worth the effort:

- God is so forgiving.
- God knows that forgiving others is good for us.
- Refusing to, damages our relationship with God.
- Forgiveness will benefit the forgiven.

Reason 1: God is so forgiving

When Jesus first commanded us to love our enemies, which must also include forgiving them, He said He wanted us to do this so that we would be seen as sons of our Father in Heaven. In this way our Lord was reminding us that we are called to resemble our Heavenly Father. We are called to bear God's family likeness and forgiving one another is one way we do this. Remember:

- We are most like animals when we kill.
- We are most like men when we judge.
- We are most like God when we forgive.

Reason 2: Forgiving others is good for us

As our Designer and Creator, God knows that refusing to forgive others harms us in many ways and one way is psychologically. People who refuse to forgive, who entertain bitter thoughts and exhibit angry attitudes toward others, often turn into bitter and angry people. They become psychological hostages to their own hate. They do not hold a grudge as much as the grudge holds them. Refusing to forgive has the power to change us psychologically and emotionally. This is what Proverbs means when it says:

> "For as he thinks in his heart, so *is* he." Proverbs 23:7.NKJ

Several times I have seen people who have been wronged but because they have refused to forgive they have became bitter to the point that they became just like the wrongdoer. If you want to become a resentful person, refuse to forgive and fill your mind with resentful thoughts and plans. You see, resentment literally means, "to feel again." This attitude causes us to cling to the past, to relive it over and over again, picking at each fresh "scab" so that the mental wound never heals. As Job 5:2 says, to worry yourself to death with resentment would be a foolish, senseless thing to do.

The two primary causes of emotional stress are:

- The failure to forgive.
- The failure to receive forgiveness.

God knows that both of these damage our spirits. He knows that the only way to heal the emotional wounds caused by others is to forgive them. God also knows that unforgiveness harms us physically. It has been linked to cardiovascular disease, hypertension, high blood pressure, and even cancer. Researchers have gathered a wealth of data lately, suggesting that chronic anger is so damaging to the body that it ranks with, or even exceeds cigarette smoking, obesity and a high-fat diet as a powerful risk factor for early death. Bitterness is a dangerous "drug" in any dosage. Your health is at risk if you stubbornly persist in being unforgiving. I think this is what God was warning us of in Proverbs where it says that:

"A cheerful heart is good medicine but a crushed spirit dries up the bones." Proverbs 17:22.

Harbouring resentment can hurt us psychologically and physically and the most obvious consequence is seen in the fact that it can also do great harm to our relationships.

At the height of the Cuban Missile Crisis years ago, as tension was building toward what could have been the outbreak of World War Three, Soviet Premier Nikita Khrushchev sent an urgent communiqué to US President John F. Kennedy. In part, the message said, "You and I should not pull on the ends of the rope in which you have tied a knot of war, because the harder you and I pull...the tighter the knot will become. And a time may come when this knot is tied so tight that the person who tied it is no longer capable of untying it. What that would mean I need not explain to you, because you yourself understand perfectly what dread forces our two countries possess."

Khrushchev was exhibiting wisdom on this occasion because in effect, when we make the decision to return evil for evil, *we are choosing* to yank on "the rope of conflict" and make the knot in our relationship so tight that it may never be able to be untied. When we forgive and simply drop our end of the rope, we reduce the tension and preserve the possibility that the knot might be untangled and our relationship restored. Hatred writes people off. Only forgiveness holds out hope that relationships can be mended and that enemies can be made into friends! There were probably Christians in the Church at Jerusalem who hated Saul of Tarsus when he was filled with malice and he was breathing threats and murder against the Church. Who would have guessed that he would become the Apostle Paul, preaching love and forgiveness? Our enemy today may become our sister or brother tomorrow. Jesus is saying that we must treat them as our brother and sister today. Relationships do not thrive because the guilty are punished but because the innocent are merciful.

Reason 3: Damage to our relationship with God

Our refusal to forgive will damage our relationship with God. Could there be more serious harm to us than this?

When we fail to forgive we sin. When we sin we erect a barrier between ourselves and God through which His love and mercy cannot flow. We tend to think that being forgiven by God and forgiving others are two separate things but they are you not. God's forgiveness of our sin hinges on our forgiving others. In Matthew 6 Jesus said:

"If you forgive men when they sin against you, your heavenly Father will also forgive you. But if you do not forgive men their sins, your Father will not forgive your sins." Matthew 6:14.

It seems obvious that a door closed from one side is closed from the other. A "door" closed from one side so forgiveness cannot get out is also closed from the other side so forgiveness cannot get in. God is willing to forgive the unforgiving but their condition is such that they are incapable of receiving forgiveness.

Leonardo da Vinci painted his famous fresco of "The Last Supper" in a church in Milan. At the time he had an enemy who was a fellow painter. Da Vinci had had a bitter argument with this man and despised him. When he got to the point of painting the face of Judas Iscariot at the table with Jesus, Da Vinci decided to use the face of his enemy. It brought him great pleasure to think that for ages to come others would equate his enemy with Judas the betrayer of Christ. As weeks passed and he worked on the faces of the other disciples, he would often try to paint the face of Jesus but could not make any progress. He had sort of a "painter's block." Da Vinci felt frustrated and confused. But in time he realised what was wrong. His hatred for the other painter was holding him back from finishing the face of Jesus. Only after making peace with his fellow painter and repainting the face of Judas was he able to complete his masterpiece.

This illustrates the fact that it is only when we forgive that we can "look God in the face", so to speak, and enjoy a close walk with Him. So you see, forgiving others is good for us. It has psychological, physical, relational and most of all spiritual benefits.

Reason 4: Forgiveness benefits the forgiven

When you forgive:

- You slice away the wrong from the person who harmed you.
- You disengage that person from his hurtful act.
- You re-create that person.

FORGIVENESS does have the power to re-create

A wonderful example of this is Peter. Remember when his cowardice led him to deny Jesus three times when Jesus had been arrested? But on the beach, the morning after Jesus' resurrection, He forgave Peter. And as a result Peter was changed, transformed! He boldly preached at Pentecost and thousands came to faith in Jesus. Peter died as a brave martyr for his faith in Jesus. God used Peter in a great way to further His Kingdom but this would not have happened if he had never been forgiven for his cowardice.

FORGIVENESS makes repentance and change possible

- The question is not 'Should I forgive if they do not repent?'
- The question is 'Can they repent if I do not forgive?'

We have dealt with the "What" and the "Why" of forgiveness but our study brings one more question to mind, "How?"

QUESTION 3: HOW can we forgive?

How can we do this thing that goes against our nature? In

his book *God's Outrageous Claims,* Lee Strobel suggests that we use the word PEACE as an acronym, to help us remember five things that make forgiveness possible. Let us look at the word PEACE:

- **P** – Pray
- **E** – Empathy
- **A** – Act
- **C** – Confess
- **E** – Example

The "P" in PEACE stands for "PRAY"

In the Sermon on the Mount Jesus said:

"...I tell you who hear me: Love your enemies, do good to those who hate you, bless those who curse you, PRAY for those who ill-treat you." Luke 6:27-28.

This should remind us that the first step in the process of forgiveness is to PRAY for the wrongdoer. This may be one of the most difficult tasks you ever undertake. But this is what we must do because praying allows us to seek God's assistance and tap into His forgiving power.

In his book, Letters to Malcolm, C.S. Lewis observes, "Last week, while at prayer, I suddenly discovered, or felt as if I did, that I had forgiven someone I have been trying to forgive for over thirty years...trying and praying that I might."

Lewis learned that without the hard work of prayer, the words, "I forgive you" are empty and powerless. He was right. You see, as we pray for the person who wronged us, we find that the hard feelings and the hurt diminish. In fact we cannot pray for a person very long and still hate them. If we pray genuinely and earnestly, we discover that we cannot help but forgive. PRAY!

The first "E" in PEACE stands for "EMPATHY".

This reminds us that in order to forgive someone we need to empathise with them. In other words, we need to go back and look at them from a different viewpoint. We need to try to understand why they did what they did. We must turn from seeing them from our painful perspective to seeing them as God sees them. This point of view helps us to realise that they have infinite value to God. They bear His image even though it is distorted and obscured by sin. When we see them as people who matter to God, they begin to matter to us.

William Barclay relates a rabbinic story that emphasises how much God values those He has created even though they sin. In this ancient tale, the angels of Heaven begin to rejoice as the waters of the Red Sea close in on the Egyptian Army and drown them as they pursue the Israelites. Amid their celebration, God lifts His hand to stop them and says, "The work of My hands are sunk into the sea and you sing"?

Those angels should have read Ezekiel 33:11 where it says that God takes no pleasure in the demise of evil people.

We need to love sinners as God does even though we hate what they have done to us. As Martin Luther said, *"To love one's enemy does not mean to love the mire in which the pearl lies, but to love the pearl that lies in the mire."*

The "A" in PEACE stands for "ACT".

To forgive we need to sidestep our feelings of revenge and act in forgiving ways. We need to act ourselves into a new way of thinking, rather than trying to think ourselves into a new way of acting. This principle of action is what Jesus was teaching in Luke 6 when He commanded us to:

"Do good to those who hate you." Luke 6:27.

"Bless those who curse you." Luke 6:28.

Jesus told us what to DO when we are hurt. He said:

"If your brother sins against you, go and show him his fault, just between the two of you. If he listens to you, you have won your brother over ..." Matthew 18:15.

- YES, we must GO to the wrongdoer.
- YES, the innocent party must initiate reconciliation.
- YES, we must do it privately.
- YES, forgiveness requires action by those who are hurt.
- YES, forgiveness is not optional.
- YES, it is a command.
- YES, Jesus never said that obedience would be easy.

While we are on the subject of peace, let us consider the matter more generally. In a selfish and materialistic world where few escape the stresses of life that invade our home, work and church lives, how do we avoid the conflicts and problems that so easily seem to arise. Even our well intentioned actions have the potential to cause resentment and misunderstanding. How do we fulfil our obligations as Christians to *"live in peace with each other"*, a phrase used by Paul in 1Thessalonians 5:13? I offer some practical advice that might assist:

- Always be prepared to act in a forgiving way even if you do not feel like it!
- If a business competitor unfairly beats you for a contract, send a note offering your congratulations.
- If a friend or family member holds a grudge, keep on acting toward them in loving ways.

- If your adversaries need help moving house, fixing a flat tyre, or need to borrow something, go to their aid.

We need to act ourselves into a new way of thinking.

The "C" in PEA_C_E stands for "CONFESS".

Part of forgiveness involves owning up to our side of the problem. And more often than not we share part of the blame. I am sure you have heard the old saying that there are three sides to every disagreement. There is A's version, B's version and the truth which lies somewhere in between. Because we are human we were "born in sin" and we have a bias towards sin. Similarly, we all have a bias towards our own innocence. The fact is that we almost always bear some blame and we need to honestly re-assess our involvement. We need to:

- Consider if our jealousy, stubbornness, ambition, or even our bad attitude has contributed to the rift.
- Admit our part of the problem.
- Pray, "It is not my mother, not my father, but it's me oh Lord, standing in the need of prayer."

Few things will accelerate the peace process more than us humbly admitting our own wrongdoing and asking for forgiveness. We need to get to the point that we can say, "I am sorry. The hurt I caused you causes me pain as well."

This will show that we want to deal honourably with the friction and that we are willing to go beyond pride and self-interest to confess our part of the responsibility.

The final "E" in PEAC_E_ stands for "EXAMPLE".

What should we do when we are unsure or have

reservations about:

- How to love an enemy?
- How to proceed?
- If we have gone far enough in our effort to be reconciled?

We should look at the example of Jesus and model ourselves after Him. You might be thinking that your problem or situation is exceptional and that I am unaware of the terrible things that you have gone through. You are right because I do not known you but I know how much you and I were forgiven and remembering that ought to motivate us to forgive those who have wronged us. The truth is we will never be asked to forgive others more than God has forgiven us. If you have trouble forgiving others remember what Jesus did for you. I have condensed the events of those awful hours to help you think about Him.

- Watch in your mind's eye as His enemies arrested Him in Gethsemane and see Him graciously heal the ear of Malchus, the High Priest's servant.
- Follow as He is marched to the High Priest's home.
- See the soldiers whip Him and feel the pain as the lashes are laid on Him.
- Be present during the night that He went through those mock trials.
- Listen to the false witnesses who testified whilst He remained silent.
- Walk with Him as He carried His cross through the streets of Jerusalem and then walk with Him to Golgotha.
- Feel the agonising pain as nails are driven into His hands and feet.
- Hear the crowd mock and jeer at Him.

Then, as He prayed for those responsible for His death, listen to His request:

"Father, forgive them, for they know not what they do." Luke 23:34.

Then you forgive. Sometimes the only way we can forgive others is to remember the need we have of God's forgiveness for our sins

I cannot conclude this chapter on forgiveness without asking is there:

- Someone you need to forgive?
- Someone who needs your forgiveness?"

If so, then I hope you will see the need to act now and forgive. Use the PEACE acronym or whatever but obey our Lord and forgive for your good and for the good of those who need to be forgiven.

In this chapter I have been addressing the need for Christians to forgive but some reading these words might not be sure about God's love for them and how the death of Jesus can bring them God's forgiveness for sin. So finally may I ask you have you:

- Experienced God's forgiveness personally?
- Confessed your sin to God?
- Asked for God's cleansing?
- Claimed Jesus as Your Saviour and Lord?

If not, I hope you will do so now.

Chapter 7   Psalm 77

Has God Forgotten To Be Merciful?

We should look at 1 Kings 19.because there is often a large gap between what we expect God to do and what we experience. I do think that giving our attention to what a man called Asaph discovered can be a real and relevant help. Think about it. There is a steady diet of books and testimonies outlining the amazing miracles that God has done. I am sure that you will be familiar with this kind of advice: *"Have you got a problem? Here is God ready to deliver you right this very moment. All that you need do is ask in faith and it will be done."* This kind of triumphal attitude is around us today but what do you do when it does not work out well?

Asaph was used to singing and talking about the power of God. In Psalm 77 he is honest enough to admit that there came a time when he almost lost his way. The great thing about his song is that he moved from despair to peace. Let us look at this Psalm.

I cried out to God for help; I cried out to God to hear me. When I was in distress, I sought the Lord; at night I stretched out untiring hands and my soul refused to be comforted. I remembered you, O God, and I groaned; I mused, and my spirit grew faint. *Selah* You kept my eyes from closing; I was too troubled to speak. I thought about the former days, the years of long ago; I remembered my songs in the night. My heart mused and my spirit enquired: "Will the Lord reject forever? Will he never show his favour again? Has his unfailing love vanished forever? Has his promise failed for all time? Has God forgotten to be merciful? Has he in anger withheld his compassion?" *Selah* Then I thought, "To this I will appeal: the years of the right hand of the Most High." I will remember the deeds of the LORD; yes, I will remember your miracles of long ago. I will meditate on all your works and consider all your mighty deeds. Your ways, O God, are holy. What god is so great as our God? You are the God who performs miracles; you display your power among the peoples. With your mighty arm you redeemed your people, the descendants of Jacob and Joseph. *Selah* The waters saw you, O God, the waters saw you and writhed; the very depths were convulsed. The clouds poured down water, the skies resounded with thunder; your arrows flashed back and forth. Your thunder was heard in the whirlwind, your lightning lit up the world; the earth trembled and quaked. Your path led through the sea, your way through the mighty waters, though your footprints were not seen. You led your people like a flock by the hand of Moses and Aaron. Psalm 77.

Some deep distress is crushing Asaph and he cannot sleep. He cannot sleep yet he is worn out. Do you know this experience? We must remember that Asaph is no mere beginner to faith. He is an experienced servant of God. He has been used in leading the Nation of Israel in its worship celebrations. Now his concern is wearing him down. It will sound familiar to you I am sure: *"Lord, if prayer does not work, what have I got left?"* He thought about 'the former days'. He can look back on a history of God being far more exciting in the past than He is at present.

Asaph is a man who believed in God but he had an unanswered question. He feels rejected and forgotten. He questioned God. Do you know that you are free to question God? Jesus asked questions of God just as He did of other people. You look back on past blessings and then you look at your present situation and you ask why there are no blessings now. Why miracles then but not now? Why comfort then but not now? Asaph's painful conclusion is that *God has changed. He is not as merciful as he once was.* As we think about Asaph's problem, let us consider together three ways of approaching God:

- Believing
- Unbelieving.
- Doubting.

Believing and unbelieving are wilful acts

You choose whether to believe or not to believe. You have to ask yourself whether you have got a reason for your belief or unbelief.

Doubt can be an honest expression

Doubt can be a process that we pass through on the way to belief. We are free to ask question of God such as:

- Where can I turn?
- What can I do next?
- Where are you God in this mess?

In committing your life to God you expect something and you can get confused when you get nothing back. God will not be displeased if we ask questions. Psalm 77 shows how one man worked his way from his questions and confusion to a point of peace. It is not unusual to go through times of trauma, testing and trial. This appears to be God's standard programme for training us to trust Him more.

Have you noticed that in the Bible Jesus usually turns up late to help? When his friend Lazarus was ill, Jesus turned up four days after his funeral. The two sisters of Lazarus could not take this in: *If only you had been here our brother would not have died.*

'If only'. How often do we find ourselves in an 'if only' and questioning attitude? Like Mary and Martha we ask:

- Where were you Jesus?
- Do you know what was happening here?

There are situations when we expect God to step in immediately and to make things better. But could our expectations be wrong? For instance:

- The sisters expected a restoration from bad health.
- Jesus expected a resurrection from death.

To have a resurrection, Lazarus must die! God says: *"It is going to get worse before it gets better because I want to do something much bigger and better."*

Whilst Asaph is asking questions and doubting, there is a sudden change. He thought:

"...the years of the right hand of the Most High.' I will remember the deeds of the Lord; yes, I will remember your miracles of long ago. I will meditate on all your works and consider all your mighty deeds." Psalm 77:10-11.

Instead of doubt and despair we read about Asaph's growing confidence. I find three questions come out of what I read here:

- What changed him so suddenly?
- What lead him back to trust and peace?
- Why did God not respond before?

If we can grasp the answers, it will be an incredible help to us for those times when we need God the most and He seems distant from us.

QUESTION 1: What changed him so suddenly?

Asaph was confused but then he started to become confident. Why? The answer is that he saw where he was heading and he drew back from it. If he was forced to conclude that God could forget him, he realised that the next step would be to say that there was no God to remember him in the first place. And he knew that he did not want to go down that road.

A very good thing for us to do in a time of doubt is to look at the end of the road we are on. When Christians have come to me because they are unsettled about what to do next and what to believe, I have found it helpful to ask them if they could live without God. Their answer is 'No.' Here is the reason. They are battling with insecurity but their problem would be much worse if they walked away from God. The Apostle Peter understood this. In John 6 we read that many of those who heard Jesus speak left Him because they did not like what He said. Jesus turned to his disciples and asked:

"You do not want to leave too, do you?" Peter answered him, "Lord, to whom shall we go"? John 6:67-68.

Peter had been thinking about it. He knew that if he walked away, he would be walking away from what mattered in life. That is how Asaph felt so he stopped himself from overreacting. How did he proceed?

QUESTION 2: What lead him to trust and peace?

Many Christians stop the slide but do not take the next two vital steps that Asaph took. The result is that they never grow or develop in their faith. What steps did Asaph take? Look at verses 11-12:

"I *will* remember the deeds of the Lord; yes, I *will* remember your miracles of long ago. I *will* meditate on all your works and consider all your mighty deeds." Psalm 77:11-12.

With those crucial words, "I WILL" Asaph caught hold of himself. He is no longer the victim of his own feelings. His mind comes into the picture.

THE FIRST STEP BACK TO TRUST AND PEACE:

Thinking comes before prayer

Previously Asaph's troubles launched him to pray *"Lord I am in a mess, help me out."* His prayer was:

- Self-centred.
- Wrapped up in self-pity.

What is wrong with beginning your prayers with yourself? The answer is obvious when you think about it. You and I only have limited horizons. Let me illustrate the danger.

There was a movie where one character stepped out of the screen into the real world and was shocked. When he was hit it hurt. When he kissed he felt. Then he climbed back onto the screen and tried to explain that to the rest of the characters but they could not take it in.

How could the rest of the characters understand what he said? Their horizon on life was so limited, it was simply not big enough for them to understand. That is why we need to stop and think. Otherwise, we will get locked into one dimension. Let us say that the help we need from God is for our physical health, our physical well being. We must move from THINKING TO PRAYER not the reverse. We must think about God first and then pray with confidence. Of course, what we must watch out for is wrong thinking about God. Before you can rebuild a house you must demolish the old building. So, let us knock down any old false ideas that have been built in our minds which do us no good.

Five false ways of thinking that must go

False Idea 1: Be healed by faith not medicine.

Visit your doctor and never ditch prescribed medication. Do you have to make a choice between God and science? Receive prayer and keep taking the tablets.

False Idea 2: The right method guarantees success

Jesus did not have fixed formula either in prayer or healing. There were times when He prayed and times when He did not. There were times when He would touch a needy person and times He would work at a distance. He might use spittle or mud, or nothing at all but His word. Do not get fooled into thinking that there is a right method. Think before you pray.

False Idea 3: Blame someone if it does not work

Some people will say that more miracles happen in the developing world than here in the West and then blame the western church for its lack of faith. Maybe our faith is weaker than theirs. Maybe God is merciful to them because of their lack of medical provision. God's works of supernatural healing are wonderful as are His gifts of medical science. Reliable results come from both means of healing.

All healing is a gift from God.

False Idea 4: "I have the power"

God used Peter and Paul in spectacular ways. But they never tried to draw attention to themselves. "Look what we can do. 3 o'clock tomorrow there will be another series of miracles for you to see." They did not do it that way. They realised that the power was in God not them. Focus on the One in whose Name you pray not the one praying for you.

False Idea 5: Blame the devil for everything

Here we must watch out for two extremes:

- A Sunday morning only religion.
- Seeing demons behind every sneeze and cough.

There is a balance that we must achieve in our thinking. We must move from thoughts that are wrong to thoughts that are right. There are two essential true ways of thinking that we must start to build in our minds.

TWO TRUE WAYS OF THINKING.

Truth 1: Healing is known alongside suffering

We note this truth in the ministry of the Apostle Paul:

- He did healing miracles but suffered terribly himself.
- On long missionary journeys, he was sometimes accompanied by Doctor Luke, a medical doctor.
- Paul's companion Timothy suffered continually from a stomach problem.
- At times Paul feared for the life of a friend.

Clearly, as Paul did not deal with these particular health problems in the miraculous way that he dealt with other such problems, we must accept that in the Bible, healing is known alongside suffering. To say that healing must always happen has had catastrophic consequences in the lives and testimonies of many unhealed Christians.

- Some Christians have felt obliged to pretend that healing has occurred when it has not.
- Others have been left with guilt because they think that they should have had the faith to get better. A false sense of guilt can so easily ruin a Christian's life as well as their physical and mental health.
- Still others will go on an endless quest for REVEREND DOCTOR ALWAYS RIGHT to come along with the formula that will heal them.

Because of these happenings, many people have become cynical about the whole subject. Some have even concluded that because what has been preached, taught and promised about healing has proved to be totally false, the Gospel that is so often linked with healing and healing missions must also be false.

Truth 2: Healing Can Make Suffering Harder

There is a truth mystery here that we should recognise and never forget. It really is that important when we are considering the subject of suffering and faith. And an understanding of this will save you much heartache, soul searching and disappointment and it will bring God's peace to your life in times of trouble.

Hebrews 11 refers to two groups of faithful men and women. The only difference between the two groups is the result of their faithfulness. The chapter begins with a list of great Old Testament heroes of faith. They are men and women who God helped and rescued. They were strong and successful because of their faith in a God who was able to deliver them. But did God always deliver those who had faith? Check out the end of Hebrews 11.

Through faith women received their dead relatives raised back to life. Others refusing to accept freedom, died under torture in order to be raised to a better life. Some were mocked and whipped, and others were put in chains and taken off to prison. They were stoned, they were sawn in two, they were killed by the sword. They went around clothed in skins of sheep or goats---poor, persecuted, and mistreated.

What do we find? People commended for their great faith in God that struggled, were persecuted, suffered and endured horrible painful deaths. As all these lived by faith, there was no difference in the lives lived by those mentioned in the first 35 verses and those that are mentioned in the last five verses. However, the writer of Hebrews notes something about this last group that is not mentioned of the former group:

"The world was not worthy of them." Hebrews 11:38.

What does that tell you and me? It is as if God was saying: *"They are too good for planet Earth. I want them to be with Me where I am."* No matter how faithful we are, God is not at our beck and call to do just as we decide, whether for ourselves or others. Healing speaks of dying well, not never dying.

It would be wrong and we might really lose out if we did not pray for supernatural healing. We would also be wrong in thinking that total healing is promised in the Bible for right now. Naive idealism leads us into unreal expectations and error. Weary cynicism boxes God in. God will give us 'tasters' of His deliverance in the here and now. The main blessing is when we are part of His New Earth and New Heaven, when we have a body just like the body of Jesus. Like Asaph we need to THINK BEFORE WE PRAY.

Asaph thought about God's actions. That is clear from Psalm 77:11. Just as we do not start with prayer but with thinking, we do not start with words but with God's actions. God's words are very helpful to comfort and console. But our faith must rest upon the deeds of God. Even at the human level, what a person does speaks so loudly that we do not hear what they say. We see this step that Asaph takes throughout Scripture. What did Jesus do when John the Baptist and Thomas had doubts?

John the Baptist was locked up in a dungeon and he was unsure about his future. He sent a message to Jesus to ask if He really was the Messiah. How did Jesus respond?

- Did He get upset with John and accuse him of a display of small faith?
- Did He confirm indignantly that He was the Messiah as John should have known all along?

No. He gave John the Baptist deeds not words. Jesus said:

"Go back and report to John what you have seen and heard: The blind receive sight, the lame walk, those who have leprosy are cured, the deaf hear, the dead are raised, and the good news is preached to the poor. Luke 7:22.

Jesus was saying: *"Tell him these deeds because he knows the Old Testament Scriptures and they predict what the Messiah will do when He comes"*.

Thomas doubted that Jesus was back from the dead. We read what Jesus required Thomas to do:

"Put your finger here; see my hands. Reach out your hand and put it into my side. Stop doubting and believe." John 20:27.

This was more than words. It was deeds. It was actions. Deeds strengthen our faith because we have real evidence. If our faith rests only upon subjective feelings within us, we will remain unsure about what we believe because feelings inside us can and do change. Deeds are timeless. Deeds are facts that remain in history. Not being sure about their beliefs is a major reason for the weakness of many a believer when a crisis hits them. We have not thought about or grasped and made our own the solid evidence of what God has done in our past. Our Salvation should have resulted in a change of lifestyle, a new way of living that pleases God, something that we could never have achieved by our own efforts.

Asaph looked back to what God had done for His people at the crossing of the Red Sea. Remembering that event, recorded in Exodus 14, released Asaph from his spiritual doubts and returned him to his previous state of trust and peace. That event happened years before his time but Asaph saw in it the sovereign control of his God over all events. You will recall that the people said to Moses: *"Have you led us out of Egypt to die here? We have the waters in front of us and the army of Pharaoh behind us. It is hopeless. We are doomed."* How many times have we said that our situation is hopeless and that we are trapped with no way out? Like those Israelites, we hit the panic button and cry out to God but at first nothing much seems to happen. But then God intervened. He got the Israelites through the sea and stopped Pharaoh's army from following them. As Asaph looked back to that amazing event he realised that he had the same God. God was no different. He was still his God. Behind every event that frightened Israel was God's Hand.

A magnificent example of God's hand in human affairs is seen when Jesus remained silent at His trial before Pilate. An indignant Pilate said to Him:

"Don't you realize I have power either to free you or to crucify you?" And Jesus calmly replied:

"You would have no power over me if it were not given to you from above" John 19:10-11.

How I wish that there was a way to impart these truths about God's ways to every Christian:

- We must be humble when we are considering God's ways. Do not forget that we are dealing with a sovereign God.
- We must admit our total inability to understand how, when and why God acts or chooses not to act.
- Humans cannot judge that God is inactive.
- Our inability to understand God's ways can never be an indication that He is inactive and it would be extremely foolish to think otherwise.

I want to make these truths crystal clear. When you have difficult problems to cope with, failure to accept these truths will add a serious spiritual problem as well. And the spiritual problem will be self-inflicted! I want to avoid that happening to you so I repeat, it is both foolish and wrong to insist or expect that God will explain Himself to us or spell out to us every move that He is about to make.

Let me show you this from the Scriptures we are

considering:

- Did God have a plan for His people before their difficulties arose? Of course! God knew exactly what He was going to do in the future before they left Egypt.
- Did God explain His plans or course of action before His people left Egypt or when they faced the problem of the Red Sea? As we shall read later, God said nothing, He was totally silent.
- Because God said nothing, did He do nothing? Of course not! He brought the Israelites safely through the Red Sea.

Look back and see how God has brought you through some very difficult or impossible circumstance. That action of God then can help you now if you will think it through. It can steady you and give you firm ground on which to stand. All this brings us to the third question we want to ask.

QUESTION 3: Why did God not respond before?

When a parent wants their child to learn to walk, you know the routine. You see the toddler. Left foot forward followed by the left foot forward and down they go. No wonder they are called toddlers! The child learns the technique little by little. When the child begins to get the hang of it and takes those first few steps, the parent starts to edge away. The child must be thinking. Why are they edging away from me? We know the answer. Parents do not want to spend the rest of their lives pushing a pram! Seriously, we all accept that the learning process cannot stop when a child can only walk one or two steps unaided. Only a foolish parent would think otherwise. If God our Heavenly Father responded instantly to our every wish, there would be no need for us to have trust and faith and we would never learn to depend upon Him.

As Asaph thought about the Red Sea incident, he realised that it was always God's intention to lead the Israelites THROUGH the Red Sea. That was God's intention before they left Egypt:

"Your path led through the sea, your way through the mighty waters, though your footprints were not seen." Psalm 77:19.

That never entered the Israelites' minds.

Though His 'footprints were not seen', that is, they could not predict how things would work out, God knew all along what He was going to do when problems arose.

Annie Johnson Flint suffered a lot in her life. She captured this truth in a wonderful poem.

Have you come to the Red Sea place in your life,
Where in spite of all you can do,
There is no way out, there is no way back,
There is no other way but through?

Then wait on the Lord with a trust serene,
Till the night of your fear is gone,
He will send the wind, He will send the floods,
But He will say to your soul, 'go on.'

And His hand will lead you through - clear through,
Ere the watery wall roll down,
No foe can reach you, no wave can touch,
No mightiest sea can drown.

The tossing billows may rear their crests,
Their foam at your feet may break,
But over their bed, you may walk dry shod,
In a path that your Lord will make.

In the morning watch, 'neath the lifted cloud,
You shall see but the Lord alone.
Where He leads you on, from the place by the sea,
To the land that you have not known.

And the fears shall pass, as your foes have passed.
You shall be no more afraid.
You shall sing His praise in a better place,
A place that His hand has made.

Unlike us, God is never taken by surprise. He does not need to fall back on Plan B or have Contingency Plans in place to deal with changed circumstances or unforeseen problems. And God does not panic and hope for the best. To be prepared for difficult times, you will need to understand that God's path out of Egypt led the Israelites:

- Through the waters of Red Sea.
- Through all the many problems that came their way.

They were not led around either of them. I repeat, it is important that we grasp this truth for our own lives.

Remember Asaph's circumstances:

- He cried out to God when he saw no hope.
- He did not hear God answer.

Remember Moses' and the Israelites circumstances:

- The Red Sea was in front of them.
- The Egyptian army was behind them.
- There was no way forward.
- There was no way back.

The Israelites called out to Moses:

"Was it because there were no graves in Egypt that you brought us to the desert to die?" Exodus 14:11.

The Israelites were desperate. However, like Asaph, they had seen God work for their blessing in their past. The plagues on their Egyptian overlords, that had gained them their freedom, had showed God's power, holiness, and redemptive love for them. But, instead of remembering past blessings, they got caught up in their present circumstances. Moses' responded to the people:

"Stand firm and you will see the deliverance the LORD will bring you today!" Exodus 14:13.

We know what Moses said to the people. However, verse 15 is interesting because God spoke to Moses:

"Why are you crying out to me? Tell the Israelites to move on!" Exodus 14:15.

Although Moses stood firm before the people to encourage them, he was actually crying to God for help for himself. And that is what Psalm 77 discloses Asaph did.

What does God say to Moses to help him in these extremely difficult and dangerous circumstances? NOTHING at all. God had told Moses before the Israelites had left Egypt that He would personally deal with the Egyptian army and that His victory over them and the Pharaoh would bring honour to Himself. So Moses could and should have relied on God to deal with the Egyptians. That left only one problem, the Red Sea. And so God gave Moses the instruction that the people were to go forward.

In Psalm 77, we read how wonderfully Asaph had grasped an essential truth about God, God's sovereign power. Let us see what he had learnt about God and how he applied his knowledge. What were the Israelites afraid of?

- ❏ They were afraid of the Egyptians.
- ❏ They were also afraid of the Red Sea.

They could not walk into the sea as humanly speaking that would have meant death for them. Yet what does Asaph say about the waters:

"The waters saw you, O God, the waters saw you and writhed [*they* were afraid]." Psalm 77:16.

This is an example of anthropomorphism. Asaph gives a personality to the waters to make the important statement that anything and everything we face in this world that causes us to fear is under the control of a sovereign God. To prove the point to us, Asaph continues:

"The clouds poured down water; the skies resounded with thunder; *your* arrows flashed back and forth. *Your* thunder was heard in the whirlwind, *your* lightning lit up the world." Psalm 77:17-18.

The lightning and thunder belonged to God and were under His control. God was in absolute control of everything that was bringing fear to the Israelites but they:

- ❏ Did not see this ahead of time.
- ❏ Only saw a barrier.
- ❏ Thought that there was no way forward.

But God's way for them was right through the Red Sea. Look at verse 19:

"Your way through the mighty waters, though your footprints

were unseen." Psalm 77:19.

The Israelites could not tell that:

- This was God's escape plan for them.
- This way was God's way.
- God was working for them in the circumstances that were causing them so much pain and sorrow.

They could not see God's footprint in all this, yet He was going to lead them through this turbulence, through this difficulty, to a tremendous victory. Their problems were self-inflicted. They need not have worried about the problems that they had to face whilst they were following God's escape plan for them. Let us think about ourselves and our problems.

These emotions and feelings of being abandoned by God, of God not answering our prayers, *will* come. If you have not experienced them, I can promise you that you will at some point in your Christian life and probably at multiple points. God tells us in Isaiah 55:

"My thoughts are not your thoughts, neither are your ways my ways." Isaiah 55:8.

It is for that very reason that we cannot fathom, we cannot understand the way God works, the way in which God works in our lives. Because God is so far above us, so much greater than us, He is incomprehensible to us. Was God there for Asaph? Yes! All night long while he was crying out, God was there and at no time was He absent. God was there but for His own sovereign purposes, He chose not to remove Asaph's sense of fear. Perhaps Asaph needed to learn to trust God at times when he wrongly thought that the circumstances around him did not warrant that trust.

God's way for us is frequently "through the sea", through the difficulties. God wants to refine us, to cause us to trust Him. We see that in the stories of Bible characters such as David, Jeremiah, Daniel, Hananiah, Azariah, Mishael, Elijah and Paul. If we learn to trust God now, we shall be prepared for future problems.

Remember that the Christian who has learned to trust God in all circumstances will not be led astray by the bogus promise or preaching that some religious experience or formula will result in health, wealth and security.

We are by nature emotional and we have feelings that respond to the circumstances of life. We can experience the joys and the sorrow that are part and parcel of life in this world. Some seem to have more than their fair share of tragedies to cope with. For some life is hard whilst others seem blessed with few problems. Just as we do not expect real marriage to conform to the story book pattern of a ceremony followed by the couple living "happily ever after", our relationship to God will have high and low points. Our emotions, our feelings will ensure that, but God will always be there for us. In times of problems, we need to hold on by looking back and remembering God's past deeds. We need to know that even when we do not sense God's presence and even when we do not feel His love, He is there.

Are you reading this at a time when there is a serious problem in your life? Let me ask you two questions:

- Have you reached the point where you feel like quitting?
- Do you feel like giving up on God?

Hold it a minute! God's plans will never be hindered by

anything in our circumstances. The smartest thing that we can do in difficult times is to keep trusting because there are positive benefits from trusting that God's plan for us is the best plan of all.

- Think about what God has already done for you.
- Think about what Jesus did on the Cross for you.

We can look back to the Cross, that incredible and amazing ACTION of God for us. If ever we want to know if God cares for us, or if He loves us, we find the answer displayed there.

Because of the Cross there will be no end to God's love for the Christian. God will always be there to help you through difficult times. But this will only be of benefit to you in your daily life if you continue to trust Him.

Chapter 8   Colossians 2:13-23

Do Not Touch?

I guess that the film *Raiders of the Lost Ark* made archaeology seem very interesting. It can of course be back-breaking, tedious work under a hot sun using only a trowel to sort through dirt inside a tiny hole. We know enough about archaeology from watching the Indiana Jones movies to know that grave robbers are the bane of archaeologists. When archaeologists unearth a crypt or grave, they are often disappointed to learn that grave robbers have long since looted many of the artefacts. In my opinion, there is a tragedy that is far worse than anything grave robbers can do. It is the tragedy of grace-robbers. And grace is more valuable than gold or silver, or the most precious artefacts.

Two thousand years ago, the Apostle Paul was in prison when he heard that false teachers were teaching a doctrine that required Christians to obey the Old Testament laws in order to be accepted by God. The theological label given to these false teachers is "judaizers" because they were telling believers that they had to live like law-abiding Jews before they could be true or real Christians. They were grace-robbers. There are those today who also deserve to be called grace-robbers. They preach, write books and gather together. They would never call themselves grace-robbers although, because they are proud of their rules and regulations, some might accept that they are "legalists". Whatever name they would choose for themselves, they have not discovered the liberating power of God's grace.

The question we are considering in this chapter is in

Colossians 2:21. Let us look at the text surrounding it in Colossians 2:13-23?

"...God made you alive with Christ. He forgave us all our sins, having cancelled the written code, with its regulations, that was against us and that stood opposed to us; he took it away, nailing it to the cross. And having disarmed the powers and authorities, he made a public spectacle of them, triumphing over them by the cross. Therefore do not let anyone judge you by what you eat or drink, or with regard to a religious festival, a New Moon celebration or a Sabbath day. These are a shadow of the things that were to come; the reality, however, is found in Christ. Do not let anyone who delights in false humility and the worship of angels disqualify you for the prize. Such a person goes into great detail about what he has seen, and his unspiritual mind puffs him up with idle notions. He has lost connection with the Head, from whom the whole body, supported and held together by its ligaments and sinews, grows as God causes it to grow. Since you died with Christ to the basic principles of this world, why, as though you still belonged to it, do you submit to its rules: "Do not handle! Do not taste! Do not touch!"? These are all destined to perish with use, because they are based on human commands and teachings. Such regulations indeed have an appearance of wisdom, with their self-imposed worship, their false humility and their harsh treatment of the body, but they lack any value in restraining sensual indulgence." Colossians 2:13-23.

PAUL'S QUESTION

Why do you submit to rules and regulations?

Paul was writing to a group of Christians at Colossae in Phrygia. The group was composed of both Jews and Gentiles. Unfortunately, the group abandoned Christian doctrines and turned to Judaism, the Jewish religion with its rules, regulations and practices that you will find recorded in the Old Testament. These rules and regulations were given by God to the Jews to ensure that the Jews became and remained a Nation that was separated to God. In fact, the Jews added several hundred of their own rules to the rules that God had given them.

The Old Grace-Robbers

These grace-robbers had taught their false doctrine to the Christians at Colossae. Paul now needed to teach the Christians the truth to save them from the serious problems that false doctrine always produces. So Paul asked them why they now obeyed such Old Testament rules as:

- Do not handle!
- Do not taste!
- Do not touch!

Paul dealt with this false doctrine by reminding the Christians of what God had nailed to the Cross of Jesus.

First, God had nailed to the Cross:

- Our sin and shame.
- Satan's power

Second, God had nailed to the Cross:

- All the Old Testament rules and regulations.

By ensuring that the Christians at Colossae fully appreciated all that the death of Jesus had achieved, Paul destroyed the false doctrine. Despite this, there are modern grace-robbers who still insist that we should still obey totally inappropriate, often obscure, rules and regulations.

The Modern Grace-Robbers

Most of the grace-robbers or legalists that you will encounter today are those who impose on Christians a whole new set of their own rules and practices and they teach that if you want God to accept you, you must obey their rules without dissent. These rules vary in severity from group to group but there is a common theme that runs through them.

You are usually required to:

- Attend at all church meetings, both on Sundays and specified weekdays.
- Give your money in specified ways.
- Read only certain translations of the Bible.
- Pray in a specified way.
- Not eat or drink specified items.
- Not fellowship with Christians who do not obey the rules.

LEGALISM

Let me define legalism. It is the attitude that we can establish or improve our standing before God by our own acts or activities.

LEGALISM IS A DANGEROUS ATTITUDE

If you think that there is anything you can *do or not do* to either establish or improve your relationship with God, you may have fallen into the trap of legalism and you may have been robbed of God's grace.

From Colossians 2:14 we are introduced to three insidious grace-robbers:

- You must do this to be saved.
- You should have the same feelings as me.
- You ought to keep the rules.

Grace-Robber 1: You must do this to be saved

It is a legitimate question to ask:

"What must I do to be saved?" Acts 16:30.

That was the jail keeper's exact question. Paul's answer tells us that we do not have to do anything. He said:

"Believe in the Lord Jesus, and you will be saved!" Acts 16:31.

- Believing is not doing:
- Believing is simply trusting.

Let me illustrate what I am saying by asking how Salvation should be spelt?

- Some would incorrectly spell Salvation as DO.
- The correct way to spell Salvation is DONE.

What a vital and eternal difference there is in these words DO and DONE.

- Some people believe that Jesus died on the cross for their sins but think that there is something for them to DO to be saved.

- Others believe that Jesus died on the cross for their sins and that He has DONE all that was necessary for them to be saved.

The Bible says:

"He is the atoning sacrifice for our sins and not only for ours but also for the sins of the whole world." 1 John 2:2.

For the sake of discussion, if you think God has already done 99.9999999% of what is necessary for you to be saved and then it is up to you to do the remaining .0000001% then you do not understand either God's grace or God's Salvation and you really need to consider your spiritual condition. Paul's heart was broken for the Colossian Christians. They were still trying to DO something to improve their relationship with God.

If you are a Christian and you are concerned by what you have read, you might wish to challenge me and ask me to clarify what I am teaching.

Let me make this clear:

- I am not saying that when you were saved you were like a robot and that you had no part in the transaction.
- You might feel that you chose Jesus to be your Saviour. You did, but Jesus chose you before you chose Him.
- To obtain God's Salvation you did have to accept Jesus as your Saviour. But before you ever accepted Him, He accepted you.

You can see the contrast that there is between the people who DO and those who rely on what Jesus has already DONE for them.

Grace-Robber 2: You should have the same feelings as me

Legalists believe that every follower of Jesus should look and act in a certain way. They teach that if you are truly right with God your experience will mirror their own special pattern. The pattern varies from group to group. It may involve dressing a certain way, talking a certain way, having some kind of "blessing" experience or even being baptised their way. As you can imagine, the list goes on.

Perhaps you have seen the Matrix movies? A man called Neo fights against an omnipotent computer trying to control the world. His opponent is a black-clad, sunglass-wearing figure known only as "Agent Smith". Because Agent Smith is computer generated, there is not just one of him, there are dozens of identical Agent Smiths fighting against Neo. That reminds me of some Christian fellowships. They would love for every Christian to talk and dress a certain way. As Billy Graham remarked about such Christians, they misread what the Lord said. They thought He said, "By their suits shall you know them". The legalists' attitude can be summarised in this poem:

Believe as I believe
No more no less.
That I am right
And no one else, confess.
Feel as I feel
Think only as I think.
Eat what I eat
And drink what I drink.
Look only as I look
Do always as I do;
Then and only then
Will I fellowship with you!

God could have created us so that we look exactly alike but He made us so different that the skin pattern on your thumb is different from the other six billion people on the planet. No two snowflakes are identical. No two sunsets are the same. Life would be boring if all Christians were identical. There is an amazing diversity and beauty in the Body of Christ!

Grace-Robber 3: You ought to keep the rules

Many Christians embrace the idea of grace for their Salvation but then fall into the trap of thinking that *after* they become a Christian, there are things that they must do to keep their Salvation alive. I must confess that I have never had a problem believing it was God's grace and God's grace alone that brought me into His Family. But I want you to know that I am a recovering legalist. For years I believed that once you were saved there were things you *must* do if you wanted to continue to receive God's favour. I thought I *had* to read my Bible and pray daily if I wanted to maintain God's love and blessing in my life. I thought I *had* to constantly witness and bring people to Christ and if I did not, I was disappointing God and letting Him down.

When you understand grace, you will *want* to obey God's commands. The difference between legalism and grace is the motive behind our obedience. If you obey God with the belief that it will improve your standing with God, or that He will love you less if you do not, then you are sliding into the gloom of ice cold legalism. If you obey God because you love Him and know you are deeply loved, then you are basking in the warmth of His grace. I do not read my Bible and pray because I feel I have to. I do these things because I want to! I do not try to share my faith with people because I feel like I have to. I do it because I know how much God loves me and I want others to know that love.

The Bible emphasises repeatedly that our relationship with God is not based upon what we do but on who He is.

"For the kingdom of God is not a matter of eating and drinking, but of righteousness, peace, and joy in the Holy Spirit." Romans 14:17.

Remember that faith has:

- NOTHING to do with WHAT goes into your body.
- EVERYTHING to do with WHO lives in your heart.

Remember also what Jesus is continually doing for us

- Jesus is our righteousness: Because we could never be good enough WITHOUT HIM.
- Jesus is our peace: Because we could never have security WITHOUT HIM.
- Jesus is our joy: Because WITHOUT HIM, we would be the most miserable of all men.

Self Diagnostic Test

Here is a test to see if you are leaning toward legalism:

- The test has only one question.
- Just answer it for yourself.

Question: How does God feel about me today?

- I am not asking you how you feel about God.
- I am asking you how you THINK God feels toward you right now.

What is your answer?

God's grace knows only one answer: GOD IS PASSIONATELY IN LOVE WITH ME. So, do not let anyone or anything rob you of the blessing of God's grace!

I now want us to examine three cheap substitutes for grace and then compare Christian fellowships based on legalism and those based on grace.

CHEAP SUBSTITUTES FOR GRACE

We all know that shadows are a one-dimensional outlines of the real thing. When we see a person's shadow around a corner in the late afternoon, we know that a person is there behind the shadow. Do we greet the shadow? No. We greet the person when we see them. There are Christians today who are still trying to please God by focusing on the shadows and not the real things. Keeping religious rules and observing religious rituals in order to be close to God are only a shadow of the "real thing," a relationship with Him through Jesus. Jesus is the substance of grace and legalism focuses on the shadowy substitutes for grace.

Substitute for Grace Number 1:

"do not let anyone judge you by what you eat or drink."
                                                    Colossians 2:16.

The Law of Moses in the Old Testament contained a long list of foods that were clean and unclean. For instance, the Jews could eat beef but they were forbidden to eat pork. They could eat fish with scales but not fish without scales such as catfish. The legalistic attitude about food and drink can go beyond what the Old Testament required. There are people around today who will try to condemn you based upon their rules about what you eat and drink.

In Matthew 15 Jesus said:

"Don't you see that whatever enters the mouth goes into the stomach and then out of the body? But the things that come out of the mouth come from the heart, and these make a man 'unclean'" Matthew 15:17-18.

What causes us to be defiled? Jesus made it clear that:

- It is not what goes INTO OUR MOUTHS.
- It is what comes OUT OF OUR HEARTS.

As we read at the beginning of this chapter, the Old Testament dietary rules were nailed to the cross and we do not have to obey them.

The Christian life is about knowing Jesus personally. It is not about food or drink. It is not even about the bread and wine for Communion.

Substitute for Grace Number 2:

"Do not let anyone judge you by what you eat or drink, or with regard to a religious festival, a New Moon celebration." Colossians 2:16.

The Hebrew lunar calendar was 360 days long, based on the phases of the moon.

Every year, the Jews celebrated four major festivals:

- The Passover.
- The Feast of weeks or Pentecost.
- The Festivals of Tabernacles.
- The Day of Atonement called Yom Kippur.

In addition, there were:

- Monthly festivals.
- New moon celebrations.
- Special celebrations every 7th and 50th year.

Legalism rears its ugly head when we take our holidays more seriously than the things they commemorate. Would I upset some of you by stating that:

- December 25th was not the actual birth date of Jesus?

    And yet I know of one legal office that had to open on Christmas day so that one employee could work. He wanted to demonstrate in a practical way his belief that Jesus was not born on Christmas Day. Would it surprise you to know that thereafter he was regarded as a religious idiot and a person to avoid at all costs? His testimony was in tatters. He resigned shortly after.

- Our English word "Easter" comes from an ancient pagan goddess?

When you think of the wonderful opportunities that Christians have at Christmas and Easter to celebrate the birth, death and resurrection of Jesus and to preach the Gospel to those who so desperately need God's Salvation, you really do have to wonder about the spiritual condition of those Christians whose rules would forbid them taking part in these celebrations. Do they not know, have they never considered that the Old Testament religious holidays were only shadows? There are no more shadows because Jesus is the Light of the world that causes the shadows to go. We shall miss so much blessing if we fail to appreciate that we should be living our Christian lives in the light and not the darkness.

Sadly, the Judaizers and those Christians that obeyed their false doctrines in Colossae were focusing on shadows when the real Lamb had come!

When we start focusing and concentrating on the holiday itself, rather than the truth behind the holiday, it will not be long before we are guilty of focusing on shadows too.

Substitute for Grace Number 3:

"do not let anyone judge you…with regard to… a Sabbath day." Colossians 2.16.

MISTAKES ABOUT THE BIBLICAL SABBATH:

MISTAKE Number 1

Some insist that the Fourth Commandment that concerns Saturday, the Jewish Sabbath, is still in effect and that:

- Christians should worship on Saturdays.
- Christians should not work on Saturdays.
- Christians are wrong to worship on Sundays.

It is extremely important to note that the Bible lists Sabbath observance in the same category as the Jewish dietary laws and holidays. If you worship on Sunday, never let anyone condemn you with regard to a Sabbath. The requirement to keep the Jewish Sabbath was nailed to the cross and God took it out of the way.

MISTAKE Number 2

It is the belief that somewhere in the Bible, Sunday becomes the Christian Sabbath, that all the rules that applied to the Jewish Sabbath have now been transferred to Sunday. There have been many who have tried to treat Sunday like the Jewish Sabbath. In the 4th Century, the Roman Emperor Constantine outlawed work on the day of the Sun, Sunday, but it was not for any religious reason. Later, and in error, it became part of official dogma that God changed the Sabbath from Saturday to Sunday.

The early church worshipped on Sunday, because the resurrection of Jesus was discovered on a Sunday morning but it is not a day more holy than any other day of the week. The Bible never directs us to treat Sunday as the Old Testament Sabbath. To save us from error, it is important that we realise that the word "Shabbat" does not mean "seventh", it means "rest." And Jesus is the substance, the reality, behind the shadow.

We do not need a Sabbath day, because we have a Sabbath Person. It is impossible to WORK for salvation. We need only rest ("Shabbat") in what Jesus has done for us on the cross. He said:

"Come to me all you who are weary and burdened and I will give you - SHABBAT - rest." Matthew 11:28.

If you ask me which day is the Sabbath, my answer will be that Saturday, Sunday, Monday, Tuesday, Wednesday, Thursday, and Friday are all Sabbath days because every day and all day long, I am resting in Jesus. I am not looking at and chasing shadows. Jesus is the substance behind the shadow!

I know from personal experience that legalism is a terrible threat to the spiritual health of Christians. It is important that Christians are able to distinguish between legalistic fellowships and grace-based fellowships and I have spent many years as a member of both.

I think I know why some Christians like their legalistic fellowships. When we follow the rules imposed on us, we can feel that we are doing well as Christians, especially when we compare ourselves to others who might not be keeping the rules to the same extent. What a miserable and dreary way of living the Christian life that should be exciting and full of joy.

CONTRASTING FELLOWSHIPS

I would like to make five contrasts between legalistic and grace-based fellowships.

Legalistic fellowships:

- Tend to be judgmental and critical.
- Consider it is important to maintain appearances.
- Create inter-personal distances.
- Emphasise external righteousness.
- Create a spirit of underlying depression.

Let us look at each of these attitudes and problems:

First: Judgmental and Critical

Members of legalistic fellowships tend to criticise each other and are antagonistic to Christians outside of their fellowship. A legalistic Christian compares himself to others and likes what he sees.

Grace-based fellowships demonstrate acceptance and a desire to help those who have problems. Grace does not ignore or minimise sin. But the attitude of grace based fellowships is not "You cannot come here until you clean up your act." It is, "How can we help you with your problems?"

Second: The Maintenance of Appearances

You really cannot be honest about your sins and struggles in a legalistic fellowship because they will disown you. If you start talking about how many problems you have, you are going to be judged faster than you can blink your speck-filled eye. Your so-called Christian friends would be the *last* people you would tell about your problems. After all, appearances must be maintained at all costs. In contrast, in a grace-based fellowship there can be honesty and transparency. People are able to be vulnerable and admit they have problems. In a grace-based church a person can tell their Christians friends that they are struggling with this or that problem and seek prayer.

Third: Inter-personal distances

In legalistic fellowships members may seem outwardly friendly. They will smile and shake your hand and may even offer you a brotherly or sisterly hug. But while legalism creates acquaintances, it seldom produces true and real friendships. You have to build walls so that no one can find out your problems. Grace-based fellowships encourage inter-personal closeness. Grace creates an atmosphere in which you can find friends who will love you warts and all. Their love goes deeper than a smile and handshake. Grace gives us the power to love and accept each other as we really are.

Legalism not only imposes a long list of irrelevant rules upon its followers, it keeps their scores as well! But according to I Corinthians 13:

> "Love keeps no record of wrongs." I Corinthians 13:5.

Fourth: They emphasise external righteousness

Legalists are interested in things like:

- The clothes you wear when you attend services.
- Which version of the Bible you read.
- How you pray.

Remember, a legalist is someone whose list of "right and wrong" is longer than God's. Grace-based congregations focus on Christ's righteousness, which is the only kind of righteousness that God recognises. The legalists claim that grace-based fellowships accept an "anything goes" kind of Christianity. Grace does not teach that there are no standards. Understanding grace gives you a desire to please God because you are loved and you love Him, not to work for or earn His favour.

Fifth: A spirit of underlying depression

On the surface, there may be a veneer of happiness in legalistic fellowships, where people "put on a happy face" but underneath there is deadness and depression. The reason is obvious. Legalists can *never* live up the standard of perfection required, so they are constantly reminded of failure. If you saw your doctor and he diagnosed that you had an ulcer, how would you react if on every visit all he did was repeat the same words, "you have got an ulcer". Before much more of that you would say, "Yes, doctor, I know I have an ulcer but please tell me what I can to do about it as I want to be healed!" If all he does is remind you of your ulcer problem, get another doctor!

It is amazing to me that some Christians can keep going to legalistic fellowships where they are spiritually beaten up week after week with reminders of their sinfulness. In stark contrast, grace-based fellowships are characterised by a spirit of release, liberty and joy. Remember:

- The law binds us but grace sets us free.
- Legalism frustrates but grace liberates.

The attitude found in a grace-based fellowship is that of sinners who have been and are being forgiven, even though they have done nothing that would merit or deserve God's grace. That kind of truth will set you free and fill you with real joy. Legalistic fellowships often teach they have the monopoly on truth and doctrine. Grace-filled churches usually acknowledge that they are not the only ones going to Heaven.

I love the scenery of Scotland. But visit at certain times of the year and you had better have some insect repellent available. If you do not, those pesky midges will feed on your flesh. Insect repellent is formulated to keep them away from you. Do you know what legalism really is? It is Jesus repellent. Legalism actually drives away sinners who are seeking forgiveness. People seeking God may go to a legalistic fellowship but when they see the list of rules they are turned off, because they think that they cannot keep them. They are seeking God but what they find is a long list of do's and don'ts. They look at strict, joyless legalists and say, "If that is Christianity, I do not want it!"

You may be thinking, "Derek, I understand the distinction that you have been making between Christians who would rob other Christians of God's grace and those who appreciate and enjoy God's grace in their daily lives.

But I need you to clarify what you have written about sinners who are seeking salvation. Are you saying that:

- We ought to make the gospel attractive?
- Grace-filled fellowships make the gospel attractive?"

NO! We do not have to make the gospel attractive because:

- It already is!
- It is good news!
- It is called "the gospel of God's grace." (Acts 20:24)

If legalism is like repellent, "the gospel of God's grace" is like smelling the fragrance of a bakery that sells fresh rolls! You cannot eat the fragrance but you can follow your nose to the place where you can buy and eat the rolls. Grace does not save you. Jesus does. But grace is the aroma that leads to Jesus. God wants to set you free from the notion that the Christian life is about:

- Special diets
- Special events
- Special days.

It is all about Christ in you, the hope of glory. Stop chasing the shadows of religious performance and surrender to Jesus who will fill you with His grace! The danger of legalism is that it reduces the Christian life to a set of rules and regulations so that when a legalist keeps the rules, he feels good about himself. It reminds me of a parody on an old nursery rhyme:

Legalist Holy Hugh
Sat in a pew
Dreaming of pie in the sky
He looked 'round the room
Mimicked the gloom
And said, "What a good boy am I!"

We should be upset about the things that upset Jesus. Legalism, which in the days of Jesus was practiced by the Pharisees, upset Him. We should be doing everything we can to eradicate it. We should learn to recognise those grace-robbers who would try to infect us with their dangerous spirit of legalism.

I heard about two dairy cows grazing alongside a highway when a tanker wagon full of milk passed by. On the side of the wagon was a sign that said, "Fresh Milk, pasteurised, homogenised, standardised, Vitamin A added." One cow turned to the other and said, "Kind of makes you feel inadequate".
Have you ever looked at the requirements of the Christian life and felt inadequate? Do words like "holiness, sanctification, perfection, blameless, or pure" scare you? It will be a great day for you when you admit that by yourself you are incapable of living the Christian life as you should do. When you admit that, you are ready to experience the wonderful liberation of God's grace.

Legalism keeps you in slavery to rules but God's grace sets you free in a love relationship. Notice two liberating aspects of grace.

Grace removes the pressure to perform

Grace tells us that God has done and will do it all. Therefore, there is no longer any pressure to "look busy" or to "work hard" hoping that God will toss us a few more favours!

I am enjoying the full riches of God's grace now and it is a liberating experience because I am not trying to get from God what I already have!

Grace frees you to enjoy your life with God

A legalist feels uncomfortable whenever you start talking about *enjoying* anything that is spiritual! But grace sets us free to enjoy a relationship rather than to endure rules.

Do you endure religion or have you an enduring relationship with God? Jesus said:

"If you love me, you will obey what I command." John 14:15.

In other words, grace-filled Christians do what He says because they love Him, not because they want to impress Him. Only the Christian faith dares to make God's love unconditional and undeserved.

In the early church, the first Christians were all Jews. When God started choosing Gentiles to be His children, the Jewish Christians were faced with a dilemma. Did Gentiles have to adopt the Jewish religion and behave like Jews in order to be Christians? Some preachers taught that unless Gentile men were circumcised they could not be saved. But in an impassioned speech, Peter said:

"Why do you try to test God by putting on the necks of the disciples a yoke neither we nor our fathers have been able to bear? No! We believe it is by the grace of our Lord Jesus Christ we are saved, just as they are." Acts 15:10-11.

The early church had to choose between two doctrines:

- The grace of God.
- The yoke of legalism.

A yoke was a harness that was put on the neck of farm animals to control them. Peter claimed that the Old Testament law with all its rules and regulations was like a heavy yoke on a Christian's neck.

In the early days of my Christian life, I lived under the heavy yoke of legalism. I thought a good Christian kept certain rules and regulations. I thought the only proper church attire was a coat and tie, and then, nothing too bright or flashy! My daily quiet time was just a part of my routine and I fulfilled it with military precision. I thought I could make God love me more if I kept these rules and regulations. I was bearing a heavy yoke around my neck. In Acts 15 Peter said it was a yoke that was too heavy for anyone to bear and I agree.

Are you still trying to obey rules and observe rituals to earn God's favour? I do not know about you but I do not want a legalistic yoke tied around my neck. I have renounced legalism in all its dangerous forms. I live in another yoke, a yoke that is not heavy at all. Jesus said:

"Come to me, all you who are weary and burdened and I will give you rest. Take my yoke upon you and learn from me, for I am gentle and humble in heart, and you will find rest for your souls. For my yoke is easy and my burden is light."
Matthew 11:28-30.

Instead of the yoke of legalism I have decided to live in the yoke of Jesus. It is a yoke designed for two. Jesus is providing all the grace and power. That is why His yoke is easy and His burden is light. He is carrying the entire load! I have still got a long way to go but I am beginning to discover God's grace in all its beauty and power.

Legalism makes the Christian life hard! The Bible says:

"The way of the unfaithful is hard!" Proverbs 13:15.

But God asks:

"Is anything too hard for the Lord?" Genesis 18:14.

Your Christian life should not consist of you trying to imitate Jesus. That would be more than hard, that would be impossible. The Christian life is allowing Jesus, who is full of grace and truth, to live His life through you. So, child of God, run as fast as your legs will take you from grace-robbers and reach out your arms to the open arms of Jesus and embrace grace and then, in the Name of Jesus, lighten up and grasp the promise that Jesus made. My yoke is EASY and My burden is LIGHT!

Chapter 9   1Samuel 17:1-51
Who Can Stand Against The Armies Of The Living God?

Seabiscuit is an old black-and-white movie. It is all about a famous little racehorse! Seabiscuit was a very small horse, less than 15 hands, about the size of a big pony. He was very unlike typical racehorses because back then the winning horses were big and muscular. Thoroughbreds were the "giants" of racehorses! But not Seabiscuit. No. In fact, when his famous trainer first saw him, Seabiscuit had a limp and a wheeze in his breathing. One thing that frustrated his first owners was the fact that even though he was small Seabiscuit ate twice as much as other horses. Another thing, unlike his aggressive peers, Seabiscuit was born with a gentle nature. His favourite pastime, other than eating, was to lie dozing under the juniper trees. Because of all these things his first owners dismissed him as not having any real value when it came to winning races. In fact they set him up to lose races as a way of giving other horses confidence. His trainer saw something in Seabiscuit and convinced his boss to buy him. He worked with Seabiscuit and this little horse went on to win all kinds of races! It turned out that He was incredibly fast, capable of amazing bursts of speed! At the starting line when another jockey leaned over and commented that Seabiscuit was a small horse, Seabiscuit's Jockey said, "Well, he is about to get a lot smaller from your perspective!" There was another scene about halfway through the movie that recounted the time Seabiscuit was pitted against a huge thoroughbred from the East named War Admiral. When both horses lined up at the starting line it seemed inevitable that Seabiscuit would lose. But once again that little horse won. As Seabiscuit's career grew so did his fame. It seemed as if the entire nation had fallen in love with this little horse.

And there is a clip in the movie that explains why they did. You see, the 1930's were a tough time in American history.

They were just coming out of the Great Depression and everyone in the nation felt as though they were facing problems that were bigger than they were. Everyone felt like an underdog so they all rooted for this underdog of a horse. They decided that if Seabiscuit could win against overwhelming odds then they could as well. So all over the nation people gathered around their radios to cheer him on as commentators described Seabiscuit's races.

We all know how those people felt back then because we all face "giants" in life. Some giants make us feel small. There are other "giants" that we are afraid of because we think we can never win in our struggles with them. We all root for the underdog whether it is a race horse, a prize fighter named "Rocky" or whatever.

Let me ask three questions:

- What is the "giant" that you are facing today?
- What is it that makes you feel like an underdog?
- What is the source of your fear?

Experience has taught me that so many people are not able to cope with the demands that modern life makes upon them and that so many of life's problems have no easy solutions. So let me mention a number of typical problems, because one might be similar to yours:

- Are you struggling with financial difficulties, a stack of bills that makes you afraid to check the mail?
- Do you battle with depression? Is that the "dark giant" that taunts you as you begin each day?
- Does the "cloud" of a health issue hover over your life, something so serious that even modern medicine cannot offer you hope of a satisfactory recovery?
- Is there a person at your workplace that makes you

hate your job, someone you have to face every day?
- Is the "giant" in your life a problem at home?
- Is your "giant" a habitual sin that you just cannot beat?

If I have not mentioned your particular "giant", what is it that intimidates you and steals your joy, hope or freedom? I want you to keep your "giant" in mind as we look at a text that I believe will help you learn how to be victorious.

Our text records the most famous underdog story of all time, when David defeated Goliath. The very mention of "David and Goliath" has come to represent any force or challenge that seems to be impossible to overcome:

- When a mistreated employee files a lawsuit against a large company they say, "David's going after Goliath".
- When a small nation stands up to a large nation they say "David's going up against Goliath".
- When a top soccer team gets drawn in a cup game with amateurs, it is billed as "David versus Goliath".

The true story that started this is recorded in 1 Samuel 17:

"Now the Philistines gathered their forces for war and assembled at Socoh in Judah. They pitched camp at Ephes Dammim, between Socoh and Azekah. Saul and the Israelites assembled and camped in the Valley of Elah and drew up their battle line to meet the Philistines. The Philistines occupied one hill and the Israelites another, with the valley between them"

1 Samuel 17: 1-3.

The Valley of Elah was a vast canyon about a mile wide. At the centre of this canyon was a streambed that divided the canyon. On each side of this streambed there was a gradual slope of about a half-mile. Camped on one slope was the Israelite Army and on the other was the Philistine army. Get that setting pictured in your mind's eye.

"A champion named Goliath, who was from Gath, came out of the Philistine camp. He was over nine feet tall. He had a bronze helmet on his head and wore a coat of scale armour of bronze weighing five thousand shekels; On his legs he wore bronze greaves, and a bronze javelin was slung on his back. His spear shaft was like a weaver's rod, and its iron point weighed six hundred shekels. His shield bearer went ahead of him"
1 Samuel 17: 4-7.

This text helps us to understand why the name Goliath has become not just a *name* but an *adjective* used to describe the "giants of life". This man was huge, about 9'9" tall! When he lifted his hands high over his head, you can imagine what an imposing creature he was. A basketball team would have loved to have Goliath play for them. The whole Philistine army looked up to him!

However, it was not just his size that made him seem so formidable. Goliath also wore the best armour of the day:

- He wore a heavy canvas-like undergarment that was interlaced with overlapping ringlets of bronze. This coat of mail went from shoulder to knee and deflected arrows and sword thrusts. The Bible says that it weighed 5000 shekels. That would have been at least 175 lbs., more than the weight of an average sized man.
- He had a bronze helmet and bronze leggings to protect his head and shins.
- He carried a bronze javelin or spear slung between his shoulders. The Bible says that the head of his spear alone weighed six hundred shekels, at least 20 lbs. Can you imagine someone strong enough to throw that?
- He stood behind his own personal "tank", powered by a shield bearer who walked before him carrying his shield that was the size of a full-grown man.

The Israelite Army did not have any weaponry like this so in view of Goliath's size and his armour it was clear that only the very foolish would willingly face him in battle.

Goliath stood and shouted to the ranks of Israel, "Why do you come out and line up for battle? Am I not a Philistine and are you not the servants of Saul? Choose a man and have him come down to me. If he is able to fight and kill me, we will become your subjects; but if I overcome him and kill him, you will become our subjects and serve us" 1 Samuel 17: 8-9.

What Goliath suggested here was a tactic used then in the Eastern world. It was a representative battle or a one-on-one fight. There was a fight like this at the beginning of the movie *Troy*. Goliath outlined the deal. He would represent the Philistines and Israelites would choose their own champion and whoever won, his army won and whoever lost, his army lost. This saved both time and lives.

Goliath did not issue this challenge once and then leave. No. His challenge went on for 40 days! Every morning and every evening for over a month he marched out from the Philistine camp, flaunting his size, strength and fighting gear and dared someone to take him on. Does Goliath remind you of your "giant"? Our "giants" do not just come once, do they? They come morning and evening, day after day, relentlessly trying to intimidate us. They never stop taunting us from across the "ravines" of our soul.

Meanwhile about ten or fifteen miles away, in the Judean Mountains, in the town of Bethlehem, David, a teenager, was keeping his father Jesse's sheep. Unlike three of his older brothers, he was too young to fight but as the weeks dragged on Jesse became worried about his sons. So he sent David to take them some food and check-up on them.

"Now Jesse said to his son David, "Take this ephah of roasted grain and these ten loaves of bread for your brothers and hurry to their camp. Take along these ten cheeses to the commander of their unit. See how your brothers are and bring back some assurance from them. They are with Saul and all the men of Israel in the Valley of Elah, fighting against the Philistines"
1 Samuel 17: 17-19.

Early the next morning David left the sheep in the care of another shepherd, gathered the bread and the cheese and headed out. Verse 20 says that as he came up over the rise he caught sight of both armies spread out on the plain below him. It must have been both exciting and frightening for this young man who had spent all of his time on lonely hillsides caring for sheep. As David got near to the edge of the Israelite camp he saw the troops lining up in battle formation and he heard the war cry and he stood there to watch. Any teenage boy would!

"David left his things with the keeper of supplies, ran to the battle lines and greeted his brothers. As he was talking with them, Goliath, the Philistine champion from Gath, stepped out from his lines and shouted his usual defiance, and David heard it. When the Israelites saw the man, they all ran from him in great fear". 1 Samuel 17: 22-24.

Now, picture this scene. David is standing there talking to his three brothers when suddenly he heard this loud cry from across the ravine. He looked and saw Goliath march across the streambed approaching the Army of Israel totally unafraid! All the Israelite soldiers took several steps back leaving David standing there alone. Apparently at first, Goliath would march out as far as the streambed that served as a boundary between both armies. But as the days passed and no one responded to his challenge he got bolder to the point that he actually walked right up to the

Israelite camp to issue his challenge. And that is what happened when David arrived. He was talking to his brothers when suddenly he found himself standing alone at the foot of this giant.

This should warn us that we cannot afford to tolerate a "Goliath." If we do, he will take over our territory. He will move into our "camp", steal our joy and take our peace. He will take our thoughts, those thoughts that ought to be on God and divert them to himself. This is why we cannot ignore the "giants" of life. No, we have to defeat them. We have to kill them. That is exactly what David did.

"[David] took his staff in his hand, chose five smooth stones from the stream, put them in the pouch of his shepherd's bag and, with his sling in his hand, approached the Philistine. Meanwhile, the Philistine, with his shield bearer in front of him, kept coming closer to David. He looked David over and saw that he was only a boy, ruddy and handsome, and he despised him. He said to David, "Am I a dog, that you come at me with sticks?" And the Philistine cursed David by his gods. "Come here," he said, "and I will give your flesh to the birds of the air and the beasts of the field!" David said to the Philistine, "You come against me with sword and spear and javelin, but I come against you in the name of the LORD Almighty the God of the armies of Israel, whom you have defied. This day the LORD will hand you over to me, and I will strike you down and cut off your head. Today I will give the carcasses of the Philistine army to the birds of the air and the beasts of the earth, and the whole world will know that there is a God in Israel. All those gathered here will know that it is not by sword or spear that the LORD saves; for the battle is the LORD'S, and He will give all of you into our hands." As the Philistine moved closer to attack him, David ran quickly toward the battle line to meet him. Reaching into his bag and taking out a stone, he slung it and struck the Philistine on the forehead." 1 Samuel 17:40-49.

Goliath's forehead was the only vulnerable spot he had when he was wearing his armour. The stone sank into his forehead and he fell face down on the ground. He was dead. He had been defeated!

"So, David triumphed over the Philistine with a sling and a stone; without a sword in his hand he struck down the Philistine and killed him." 1 Samuel 17:50.

As I wrote earlier, we all face "giants" in one form or another in life. In fact "giants" always seem to show up whenever we are on the way to fulfilling God's purpose in our lives. Unfortunately many of us never become all we could be for God because we allow the "goliaths" of life to defeat us. Many Christians never achieve the potential in their lives because they never conquer the things that they fear. We must learn how to defeat these huge foes that tower over us. David's example shows us three essential skills that we need to win the victory: We need

- To have good eyesight.
- To be good at dealing with criticism.
- To have a good memory.

ONE: We need good EYESIGHT

In other words, you and I have to be able to *see* our "goliaths", whatever they are, from the clear perspective of God's limitless power. This perspective enables us to "see" that God is infinitely bigger than any foes that we face. Think of it this way. To defeat the "giants of life" we do not need self-confidence but GOD-CONFIDENCE. We need to be able to perceive reality through the "lenses" of our faith in God's might, wisdom and love. It was this skill that led David to ask the question that serves as the title of this chapter. David looked at this "giant" and said:

"Your servant has killed the lion and the bear; this uncircumcised Philistine will be like one of them, because he has defied the armies of the living God." 1 Samuel 17:36.

His comment is really a reprimand. He was saying to all the troops in earshot, "Open your eyes! You are in GOD'S army! What are you doing cowering in fear?" We need to be able to grasp this comforting fact as well for we are also in God's army. David could see that in spite of Goliath's size, strength and armour, he was nothing compared to God.

The Israelites cowered because they did not have David's eyesight. Goliath had been shouting his challenge twice a day for 40 days. There is no record of anyone in the Israelite army even mentioning God before David did. In contrast, that fact that Goliath had challenged "the armies of the living God" was David's first thought!

The soldiers, King Saul included, were spiritually blind. They looked at Goliath and said, "Look how much bigger he is than us." But David looked at Goliath and said, "Look how much smaller he is than God." The Israelites said, "He is too big to hit." David said, "No. He is too big to miss." As I picture it, David stood there and said, "The only "giant" in my life is God. To conquer the "giants of life" we need eyesight like this. We must "see" for ourselves that what John wrote was not a cliché but a statement of fact:

"...the one who is in you is greater than the one who is in the world." 1John 4:4.

Our spiritual eyesight needs to be such that we can visualise our God as Isaiah described Him. Do you remember his perception of God? Isaiah wrote,

"Who has measured the waters in the hollow of His hand, or with the breadth of His hand marked off the heavens? Who has held the dust of the earth in a basket, or weighed the mountains on the scales and the hills in a balance?" Isaiah 40:12.

I am reminded of the lyrics to a song our children sang when they were young:

"My God is SO big, SO strong and SO mighty.
There is nothing my God cannot do!"

Evil has a way of deceiving us, much like those trick mirrors at the fairground. When we look at the bad that is coming our way it looks bigger than it really is. This is why it is so important for us to have an accurate understanding of God's nature and power. I am convinced that the way we live is a direct consequence of our perception of the size of our God. Think about it. When we wake up in the morning what happens if we believe in a "small" God? We live in a constant state of fear and anxiety because everything depends on us. We feel exposed and weak and vulnerable to the "giants of life".

If we believe in a small God, then when we have an opportunity to share our faith we do not take it because we think that success depends on us. If we believe in a small God, we will not be generous in giving to people who need help because we believe our financial security depends on us. We may try to get credit for something at work that we have not done because we do not trust in a big God who sees in secret and will one day give rewards.

When we shrink God we:

- Offer prayer without faith
- Work without passion

- Serve without joy
- Suffer without hope.

These things result in fear, retreat, loss of vision and a failure to persevere. David did not suffer from any of these problems. No, he had the ability to see as God sees. Goliath did not intimidate him. No matter how big the giant might be, the shepherd boy could see that God was bigger.

I wish more of us had David's vision. Think of the difference it would make in our individual lives and in our churches as a whole if we could see clearly enough to understand how big God is! I pray that, as Paul put it in Ephesians 3, we all:

"...have [the] power, together with all the saints, to grasp how wide and long and high and deep is the love of Christ, and to know this love that surpasses knowledge, [I pray] that you may be filled to the measure of all the fullness [the bigness] of God." Ephesians 3:18-19.

Remember fellow Christian, we must never look at our present circumstances and conclude that what we actually SEE is all there is to be seen. No matter what life looks like at this moment, no matter how much it appears that evil is winning, humans do not have the last word. Our Almighty God does! And His word is always a word of hope, peace and victory to those who love Him and who are walking in His will.

TWO: We need to be good at dealing with criticism

As David began to prepare to face Goliath, his elder brother Eliab confronts him. Eliab says:

"Why have you come down here? And with whom did you leave those few sheep in the desert? I know how conceited you are and how wicked your heart is; you came down only to watch the battle." 1 Samuel 17:28.

Remember, Eliab was the eldest brother and when Samuel came to Jesse's house to anoint the next king, he had been passed over. His little brother David had been chosen instead. I am sure this irritated him. So instead of doing his duty by attacking Goliath, Eliab attacked his brave little brother. Take a moment here to remember some of the characteristics of critics.

First, critics tend to be obsessed with the trivial

David was about to attempt to destroy a major threat to Israel's National Security and his brother referred to the few sheep that David normally protected. That is the way it is with critics. They seem to have an amazing ability to focus on the trivial and neglect the crucial. The fact is that we need to choose our battles wisely. If we get careless, we will get sidetracked and spend our time arguing about sheep. Meanwhile the real enemy of our souls will roam around our territory winning victory after victory.

Second, the humiliation factor

Critics attack faith-fuelled people in a hateful way because they are doing what the critics should be doing.

I agree with what George Bernard Shaw wrote, *"Hatred is the coward's revenge for being humiliated."* Criticism serves as a smoke screen to make it less obvious that the critics are not accomplishing anything themselves.

Francis Asbury, an 18th century Methodist Bishop, was criticised by a woman for being unsophisticated in his method of evangelism. Asbury politely asked the lady how many she had led to Christ. The lady answered that she had not personally led anyone to faith in Christ. Asbury's response was, *"Ma'am, I like my way of doing it better than your way of not doing it."*

David's response to the criticism of his jealous, cowardly brother was to ignore it. David's example shows us that the best way to deal with our faithless critics is to ignore them and their inaction and instead focus on the task at hand.

To defeat the "giants of life" you have to have good eyesight and be good at dealing with criticism. Then there is one more thing you need.

THREE: We must have a good memory

Think of it this way. You not only need good eyesight, you also need good hindsight. I mean this. You have to look back and remember all the ways that God has been faithful to you. Hindsight gives us insight. David remembered the "giants" God had enabled him to defeat in the past and this gave him the faith and the confidence to know that God could more than handle Goliath.

Saul heard of David's vow to kill Goliath and he called for him. Saul shows his own poor eyesight when he says:

"you are not able to go out against this Philistine and fight him; you are only a boy, and he has been a fighting man from his youth." But David said to Saul, "Your servant has been keeping his father's sheep. When a lion or a bear came and carried off a sheep from the flock, I went after it, struck it and rescued the sheep from its mouth. When it turned on me, I seized it by its hair, struck it and killed it. Your servant has killed both the lion and the bear; this un-circumcised Philistine will be like one of them, because he has defied the armies of the living God. The

LORD who delivered me from the paw of the lion and the paw of the bear will deliver me from the hand of this Philistine." Saul said to David, "Go, and the LORD be with you."
1 Samuel 17:33-37.

Had Saul forgotten what God had done in the past for the Israelites? God had never let them down. Over hundreds of years they had defeated their enemies.

So often when facing our own "giants", we forget what God has done for us too. To defeat the "giants of life", we need a good memory. We need to discipline ourselves such that we always look back and see that God has been faithful to us in the past because that hindsight will help us to have the insight we need to believe that He will do the same in the future.

As we let God defeat our "giants", we will begin to obey Deuteronomy 20 where it says:

"Do not be fainthearted or afraid; do not be terrified or give way to panic before them. For the Lord your God is the one who goes with you to fight for you against your enemies to give you victory." Deuteronomy 20:3-4.

Chapter 10   Exodus 3 & 4

What is That in Your Hand?

I am sure you would agree that in our fast-paced society free time is a precious thing. We tend to carefully pick and choose what we will do with it. When faced with the choice of what to do on Sundays, many choose not to attend church. The same inconveniences and excuses that they cite as the basis of their rationale for not attending church do not seem to impede their attendance at other things, like a football game. To show you what I am talking about let me share an article from a Christian tract. It showed how ridiculous many excuses for not attending church really are. It applied these same excuses to a professional sporting event. I got a kick out of it and perhaps you will as well. But here is how it would sound if people applied their favourite excuses for not going to church to their decision not to go to something like a football game:

- Every time I went, they asked for money.
- The people I sat next to did not seem very friendly.
- The seats were too hard and uncomfortable.
- The coach never came to see me.
- The referee made a decision I disagreed with.
- Some games went into extra time and I was late home.
- The band played music I have never heard before.
- The games are played when I want to do other things.
- My parents took me to too many games.
- Since I read a book on football, I feel that I know more than the coaches anyhow.
- I do not take my children because I want them to choose what sport they like best when they grow up.

All humour aside, the truth is that we are very good at

coming up with excuses as to why we do not do certain things for the Kingdom of God. We are asked:

- To teach a Sunday School class.
- To serve on a church committee.
- To take our turn in the Sunday crèche.
- To share our faith with a friend or a neighbour.
- To assist someone with a physical need.

In each of these instances the excuses start. We soon become experts at rationalising why we cannot give God a "yes" when He calls. Our excuses pile up until we get to the point that we never do anything for God.

The "hero" of Exodus 3-4 gave several excuses, a pile of them in fact, as to why he could not do the task God asked him to do. I am referring of course to Moses. He was originally a "Prince of Egypt." Thanks to God's protection, in a time when the Egyptians were trying to kill all the male Hebrew infants, Moses had been rescued from the Nile, adopted by the Pharaoh's daughter and then raised and educated as part of the Royal Family. The first couple of chapters of Exodus and Acts 7 tell us that when Moses grew up and saw the misery of his people who laboured under the cruelty of the slave-masters, well, he took matters into his own hands and murdered an Egyptian who was beating a Hebrew.

When the Pharaoh found out about this he tried to kill Moses. So Moses fled and went to live in Midian where he married Zipporah and started a family. He worked as a shepherd for Jethro, his father-in-law, for 40 years.

God's call to Moses came on an ordinary day. From that point on in his life nothing was ever normal or ordinary for him again. On this day God spoke to him and in so doing broke a 400-year silence. Let that sink in. During his four decades in Midian we have no record of God speaking to Moses, not even once. But, on this amazing, pivotal day, a day that was to change Moses' life and that of so many others, it dawned, just like every other day in the wilderness of Mount Horeb. I mean, no angel stopped by to tap Moses on the shoulder the night before and say, "Hey, Moses, pay attention tomorrow, because God is going to be talking to you. By the way, take my advice. Keep your eye out for unique bushes." No, there were no hints, no premonitions and no special signs to alert Moses to the fact that God Himself was about to call and change his life forever. It was just an ordinary day for Moses that he would spend with his father-in-law's sheep. The sun came up, the sheep grazed and Moses chalked off maybe his 14,600th day as Jethro's assistant shepherd.

I think that this is important for us to note because it is how God works. Without warning He speaks to ordinary people, people like you and me, on ordinary days. It could happen tomorrow. You could be sitting in the rush hour traffic, facing a classroom of 7-year-olds, climbing into your haulage lorry, crouching underneath a leaking sink, lifting your baby out of the crib, or driving your car. Whatever your ordinary routine is, that is the potential Mount Horeb in your life. It could be on just such a normal, standard-issue day that God chooses to speak to you as He has never spoken before because many times that is the way He works.

Consider our Lord's Second Coming. In Matthew 24, Jesus says that it will be just like it was in the days of Noah:

"For in the days before the flood, people were eating and drinking, marrying and giving in marriage, up to the day Noah entered the ark; and they knew nothing about what would happen until the flood came and took them all away." Matthew 24:38,39.

Jesus' Second Coming will happen like the flood did on an ordinary day when folk are doing the normal, ordinary things that the verse mentions. In the midst of our typical daily tasks suddenly Jesus will return. There will be a flash in the sky, a shout, and the blast of a trumpet and in the twinkling of an eye it will be all over with no previous warning. It will just happen on an otherwise normal day.

That is God's method. He does not need a Public Relations Department or a slick advance team. His plans do not require a drum roll or crashing cymbals. He does not use neon signs blinking, GET READY! TODAY'S THE DAY I DO SOMETHING BIG IN YOUR LIFE!" No. God works by stepping into an ordinary day and saying what He wants to say.

That is exactly what happened to Moses. This 80-year-old shepherd was kicking his sandals in the sand as he had done on countless other days, watching the sheep eat and baa and bleat when he noticed a very extraordinary thing. He saw a common desert scrub brush on fire and of course that in itself was not all that odd because like all shepherds Moses had seen lightning strike scrub brush and it had ignited. But this brush fire was unique because it did not burn out. The bush did not burn up leaving only smoke and ashes. No, it was burning with a consistent blaze that was somehow inextinguishable. There usually was not much to tell his wife about at the end of a long day of shepherding, so as verse 3 says, in curiosity he turned aside and he went over to investigate.

This is also God's method. Many times on ordinary days He does something extraordinary to get our attention, something to intrude into our routine and say, "Wait a minute. Stop what you are doing and listen. I have something to say to you." Take my advice. Whenever you come across an unusual event it would be wise to ask, "Is God trying to tell me something here?" I mean, unusual things do not just happen. Ours is not a random, whistle-in-the-dark world. There is a God-arranged plan for this world of ours, which includes a specific plan for you and me. So God does unusual things to get our attention. We must listen as He teaches us an important truth or invites us to join Him in some aspect of His work. Note this:

- When was it that God spoke to Moses?
- When was it that God issued His verbal invitation to him?

God spoke only after Moses turned aside:

"When the LORD saw that he had gone over to look, God called to him from within the bush, "Moses! Moses!" Exodus 3:4.

God will not speak until He has our attention. In the midst of our ordinary busy schedules does God need to ask us:

- What will get our attention?
- What will finally persuade us to stop our frantic living long enough to turn aside and listen to Him?

What will it take before we say, "I am going to check this out. I am going to find out what God is saying to me." Let us turn aside and do a little self-evaluation. Ask yourself:

- How good am I at turning aside?
- How hard is it for my Heavenly Father to get my attention?

Here is some pastoral advice. Learn the discipline of daily

turning aside and taking a moment to listen to God because He really does want to speak to us. Make this a normal part of your day. When you are at work, once or twice during the day, plan to take five minutes and turn aside. Take time to be still and know that God is God. Make whatever effort it needs to listen to our Heavenly Father. Pray the words young Samuel did:

"Speak LORD, for your servant is listening." 1 Samuel 3:9.

Do this because God really does long to meet with us. But just like Moses, we have to turn aside before He will speak. Moses turned aside and when he did he came face to face with his destiny. God commenced speaking to him:

"I have indeed seen the misery of my people in Egypt. I have heard them crying out...and I am concerned about their suffering." Exodus 3:7

God said "I have seen My people weeping in the night. I have heard the crack of the whip and the cries of the little ones. I have seen the bodies along the road or flung into the Nile like so many beasts of burden. None of this escapes my notice. I am going to do something about it."

I am sure Moses thought, "Great! It is about time!" but maybe he felt neutral at this point because in his mind this great thing that God was going to do did not involve him. So, as he was glowing in the joy that God was going to free His people, Moses heard the words that would change his life forever. God said:

"So now, go. I am sending YOU to Pharaoh to bring my people the Israelites out of Egypt." Exodus 3:10.

In my mind Moses did a double take and said, "What did

you say? Could you repeat that last part? ME? You are sending ME?" And of course the answer was yes! How would that make you feel? You begin to get the idea of how overwhelmed Moses felt. God was calling him to go from being a shepherd of sheep to being a shepherd of an entire Nation. I am sure that this bowled Moses over and led to his pile of excuses, excuses that can be summarised in two questions that he asked God.

Moses' first question to God

"Who am I, that I should go to Pharaoh and bring the Israelites out of Egypt?" Exodus 3:11.

I think the thoughts and questions that raced through the mind of Moses might have gone something like this:

- What will people think if I show up and try this?
- Why should they believe me?
- I cannot do this God, I am a failure! Why, in the past forty years I have not even been able to scrape together enough shekels to buy my own sheep. I still work for my father-in-law! I am a loser!
- On top of that, I am a convicted murderer and a fugitive from the law. If I go into Egypt I will be arrested and executed.
- And even if by some miracle they do not recognise me, I cannot walk into the Pharaoh's Royal Court in this outfit smelling like sheep.
- I am not so old that I have forgotten how those people look at shepherds like me. Why, the Pharaoh will laugh so hard he will fall off his throne before I even get a chance to say anything.
- I used to be important but now I am a nobody.
- Why give ME this job?

- And do not forget, I tried this deliverance thing 40 years ago and I was neither believed nor listened to then. Why should the people of Israel listen to me now?
- Why me Lord?"

So Moses' first pile of excuses added up to the fact that he felt inferior. He felt a failure. The Bible also tells us that he felt incapable. He also added to his excuse pile by saying:

"...O Lord, I have never been eloquent, neither in the past nor since you have spoken to your servant. I am slow of speech and tongue. Exodus 4:10.

Today he would have said something like, "O Lord, I am not one of those people who can sell refrigerators to Eskimos. I have never been eloquent, neither in the past nor since you have spoken to your servant." This was not entirely true. Acts 7 says that earlier in his life, during his days as a Prince of Egypt he was:

"...educated in all the wisdom of the Egyptians and was powerful in speech and action." Acts 7:22.

But that was half a lifetime ago. At this point in his life Moses thought that those years in Egypt were the "golden years" of his life. Now, he felt washed up. In his mind, he was just an old shepherd. His current skills in public speaking were limited to the words and sounds that he used to motivate sheep, not people, not a Nation, not a Pharaoh! Moses summed it all up: "I am not as qualified as others. Send someone else."

I love the way the Modern Language Bible translates it. In this version Moses said, "O Lord, please send ANYONE else!" Basically Moses said, "Anyway you look at it God, I am not qualified. So why give me this task. It makes no sense. Surely You understand that I should be excused from this task?" We need to pay close attention to all that Moses said because so many times we excuse ourselves from answering God's call with the same basic rationale:

- Why me?
- I am not talented enough.
- I am just not able to do this, God.
- No one will listen to me.
- Sorry, but You better get someone else, God.

When it comes to accomplishing God's will, these are not an issue:

- What we are.
- What talents we have or do not have.

And this is so whether God's will for us means:

- Sharing our faith with a perfect stranger.
- Teaching the Bible to children.
- Helping a neighbour in need.
- Or whatever.

Thanks to God's grace, failure was not an issue for Moses and neither was his:

- Sin and guilt.
- Limitations.
- Shortcomings.

What applied to Moses then, applies equally to us today. Why were his problems not the ultimate consideration? God's answer to this question enables us to understand why God can use ordinary people like us to do His will. Because God promised that He would be with him. In
174

essence God told him, "You are what you are but you are not yet what you are going to be!" God's promise:

- I will be with you.
- I will empower you.
- I will help you speak and tell you what to say.

As Major Ian Thomas puts it, *"Any old bush will do as long as God is in the bush. All you have to be is available"* or, to keep with the bush metaphor, all you have to be is "flammable." It was as if God was saying to Moses:

- You will burn for me like no man has burned before.
- I want you to be MY burning bush!
- You have been dried out and well seasoned in this howling wasteland for the past 40 years.
- I wanted you dried out, so that now you can burn with MY presence and power.
- You will be the 'suit' of clothes that I will wear to lead my people.

God is still looking for available, dried out people like Moses who will say:

- I am here Lord and I am yours...thorns and all.
- Just set me afire.
- This little light of mine. I am going to let it shine!

I love the words of this lyric written by Amy Carmichael:

Give me the Love that leads the way,
The faith that nothing can dismay,
The hope no disappointments tire,
The passion that will burn like fire,
Let me not sink to be a clod;
Make me Thy fuel, flame of God.

We used to refer to truly devoted followers of Jesus as Christians who were "on fire for God." Perhaps we should resurrect that phrase because the world needs Christians who burn with the love of God, believers who are passionate to do the will of God.

Well, Moses' first excuse was to ask "Who am I?" And God said "that does not matter" because:

- I will be with you.
- I will give you the power.
- I will be the fire and you will be the fuel.

I will use you but I will do this. I will:

- Stretch out *My* hand and strike the Egyptians.
- Make them favourably disposed toward My people.
- Lead My people to a land flowing with milk and honey.

I will do all this. You are just the vessel.

Well, God's response to Moses led to his second pile of excuses, excuses that can once again be summarised in the second question that he asked God.

Moses' second question to God

"Who are You?" "Suppose I go to the Israelites and say to them, 'The God of your fathers has sent me to you,' and they ask me, 'What is His name?' They will ask, 'Which God are you talking about?' Well, Who are You? What shall I tell them?"
Exodus 3:13.

Moses reversed the first question in which he asked, "Who am I that You would send me?" He now asked, "Who are You that You would send me?" Moses knew that to pull this off he would need an authority, a name that was bigger than his own. One thing his horrible failure forty years earlier had taught him was that he needed an authority beyond himself. Though his own name had once been great to the Egyptians it did not carry enough clout to convince his own people, the Israelites, that he was to be their deliverer. So he knew he needed to have a "name" far more powerful than his own. God's answer was almost as dramatic as the burning bush:

"I am Who I am' This is what you are to say to the Israelites: Tell them, 'I Am' has sent me to you'" Exodus 3:14.

In these two words, God told Moses that He is the eternally existing One, always present to help His people. God also reminded him of what He had already said to him which was:

"I am the God of your father, the God of Abraham, the God of Isaac and the God of Jacob." Exodus 3:6.

In other words, God was saying to Moses:

"I am the covenant God of the past"

"I have indeed seen the misery of my people in Egypt. I have heard them crying out because of their slave drivers, and I am concerned about their suffering." Exodus 3:7.

These words would mean to Moses:

- ❏ I saw you in the reeds of the River Nile as a baby.
- ❏ I saw you flee as a fugitive.
- ❏ I have been here with you in the desert all these years.

This was a wonderful way of saying to Moses:

"I am the compassionate God of the present"

"I have come down to rescue them from the hand of the Egyptians and to bring them up out of that land into a good and spacious land, a land flowing with milk and honey." Exodus 3:8.

This would mean to Moses:

"I am the consummating God of the future"

This is what God was saying in that two-word title. He was describing Himself as the great I AM, the eternal God in terms Moses could understand. The God Who not only knows everything but the God Who really cares about what we go through. Make sure that you take note of this. God does see all. He knows right down to the final nub exactly where you are in life. He even knows all your secret fears and your worries. God sees all and He cares! He cared about Moses and He dealt with Moses' excuses by giving him a glimpse of His power. Listen to the conversation and picture the scene!

God: "What is that in your hand Moses"?
Moses: "It is just a rod."
God: "Throw it down Moses."
Moses: "Do you mean like on the ground"?
God: "Yes, I said throw it down Moses."

- So Moses threw His rod on the ground.
- The rod became a hissing snake. Did that remind Moses of the image of a viper on the Pharaoh's crown? But this was no image, it was a live snake and God told Moses to pick it up.
- The snake became his rod.
- Then God told Moses to put his hand in his robe and take it out.

- When he did, his hand was covered with leprosy.
- When he put his hand back in his robe it was healed.

God showed Moses that He had the power to do whatever needed doing. Moses had no more excuses. In view of what he had heard God say and see Him do, how could Moses ever say no to God again? Moses said yes and God used Him in an amazing way. An entire Nation was freed from bondage and the world was changed forever. Doing all that Moses did was only possible when he was willing to let go of his doubts concerning his own and God's inadequacy.

As long as Moses held on to the belief that he was not talented enough to lead the people or as long as he held on to his doubts about the true nature of God, he would remain a shepherd. But when he let go of these feelings, when he threw them down as he did his rod, Moses became the rod of God.

What response is there from us as we have read this marvellous account of Moses and the burning bush?

- What excuses do we make when God calls us?
- Is there a "rod" that we lean on to rest when we should be working for God?
- What keeps us from putting our full trust in God?
- Have we a trust that is strong enough, deep enough to do whatever God asks?

I love the last few lyrics of that song:

What do you hold in your hand today?
To what or to whom are you bound?
Are you willing to give it to God right now?
Pick it up...let it go...throw it down.

The interesting thing about this passage of Scripture in the Book of Exodus is that it does not tell us what happened to the burning bush. We find out what happened to Moses and the children of Israel. We find out what happened to the Pharaoh and his soldiers. We never find out what happened to the bush because I think there is a sense in which it is still burning. God is still waiting for people to turn aside. I think God is waiting for that to happen right now.

Chapter 11　　　　　Genesis 3:1-21

Where Are You?

A malaria outbreak was devastating Borneo's Dayak people. The World Health Organisation was concerned and sprayed all the thatched roof huts with DDT. This however affected the natural order of things. It certainly killed off the mosquitoes but it also killed the wasps that kept down the thatch-eating caterpillars. So, the peoples' homes were being ruined. Furthermore, Geckos ate the mosquitoes and became sick. Cats ate sick Geckos and died. With no cats the rats were taking over and there was a real danger of vast numbers of people being wiped out by a deadly bubonic plague. What should be done? The answer was 'Operation Cat Drop'. I tell you the facts when I say that 14,000 cats were parachuted in. Can you imagine that scene? I guess they hit the ground feet first! It did the trick!

There is a natural order in the affairs of this world. If one thing goes wrong it has consequences. What is true in the *natural* order is also very true in the *spiritual* order of things. God wants our lives to run well and on track with Him. When we take a step away from His ordering there are consequences. We miss the positive walk that we can have with Him now and we could miss out eternally if we do not get back on track with Him. Why does it work like this? Some of the most important information we can ever learn is found in Genesis 3. People want to know:

- Why does tragedy or sorrow hit us?
- Why blood sweat and tears?

Here in Genesis is the answer. Something has happened with long lasting consequences. Perhaps you have heard the world's shortest poem entitled, "Troubles" and the poem goes: *"Adam had 'em."* And that is right. Adam had a lot of trouble. When sin entered his life, all the trouble began. We are going to think about four different events in Adam and Eve's lives:

- The dangerous conversation.
- The destructive choice.
- The divine confrontation.
- The detailed condemnation.

There are key lessons we need to learn so that we avoid the consequences of forfeiting God's blessing in our lives.

FIRST: THE DANGEROUS CONVERSATION

Satan speaks to Eve

"Now the serpent was more crafty than any of the wild animals the Lord God had made. He said to the woman, 'Did God really say, 'You must not eat from any tree in the garden?' The woman said to the serpent, 'We may eat fruit from the trees in the garden, but God did say, 'You must not eat fruit from the tree that is in the middle of the garden, and you must not touch it, or you will die.' 'You will not surely die,' the serpent said to the woman. 'For God knows that when you eat of it your eyes will be opened, and you will be like God, knowing good and evil.'" Genesis 3:1-5.

Eve got into a lot of trouble when she entered into a dangerous conversation with Satan. Satan is the tempter and the very best thing you can ever say to Satan is exactly what the Lord Jesus said to him when He was tempted:

"Get thee behind me, Satan!" Luke 4:8 KJV.

If you ever enter into a conversation with Satan you are already headed for trouble. Notice several things about this dangerous conversation.

Notice the tempter

Who was this serpent that came to Eve in the Garden of Eden? The word serpent in Hebrew is the word which means: "Shining one, beautiful one." When you think about a serpent, you probably think of some hideous creature slithering across the ground and whenever you look at it you say, "Horrible! But, at that particular time, the word serpent described a beautiful, shining creature. In fact, it was the most beautiful of all the shining creatures. Another name for Satan is Lucifer, meaning: "Bearer of light." We know that at one time, Lucifer was a powerful angel. That is who is personified in "the serpent".

Some people have read this and said, "I have heard all the stories but where in this passage of Scripture does it say that the serpent is Satan? Could it be another evil creature because it does not say Satan, it says the serpent?" Let me explain. This is an example of how the Old Testament is explained by the New. In the Book of Revelation we read:

"the great dragon was hurled down - that ancient serpent called the devil or Satan, who leads the whole world astray. He was hurled to the earth, and his angels with him." Revelation 12:9.

So we know from Scripture that the tempter in Genesis 3 is Satan. What does Satan want to do to us and why is he so interested in us once we have become Christians? What should we know about him?

- ❏ He wants to turn us away from God.
- ❏ He wants to persuade us that we should not live close to God and that living close to God is not the best way for us to live.

So, Satan is a liar because the best way for us to live is to live close to God. Always be aware that Satan has not changed. Jesus said about him:

"...for he is a liar and the father of lies." John 8:44.

But that is not all that we should know about Satan. Jesus also said about Satan that he was a murderer:

"He was a murderer from the beginning...." John 8:44.

So not only is Satan our powerful enemy, we are warned from the lips of Jesus Himself that Satan is a liar and a murderer. Satan wants to:

- Kill our joy.
- Kill our purity.
- Kill our purpose in life.

We have to face the fact that Satan has it in for us because he hates us as he hates all those who belong to God. As much as God loves you Satan hates you.

Do not think Satan will come to you in long, red underwear, or with pointed horns and a pointed tail and a pitchfork. Satan will not look like the demons portrayed in the movies. He is not some ugly creature. He came to Eve as a very beautiful creature.

The Apostle Paul says that Satan:

"...masquerades as an angel of light". 2 Corinthians 11:14.

So when Satan comes whispering in your ear, do not look for a hideous-looking demon. Satan will always be very beautiful and appealing.

Notice the target

Eve! Eve had been created from Adam and Satan waited until Eve was all alone. Never forget that whenever you isolate yourself, you become an easy target for Satan. There really is safety in numbers. What I mean by that is simply this. You must surround yourself with a lot of Christian friends. Do not be out there on the edge all by yourself. The Apostle Peter wrote:

"Be self-controlled and alert. Your enemy the devil prowls around like a roaring lion looking for someone to devour. Resist him, standing firm in the faith…" 1 Peter 5:8-9.

Watch an animal documentary and you will see how lions approach a herd of antelope. The lions are very shrewd. They do not just jump in the middle of that herd. They separate one weak antelope from it. Then they drive that antelope away from the safety of the herd and pounce on it. Heed the warning and do not get isolated from Christians. Also, if you fall in with the wrong crowd, you will become an easy target for Satan. There will certainly be no safety in numbers with them.

Notice the tactic

Satan's first recorded words in the Bible are:

"Did God really say, 'You must not eat from any tree in the garden?" Genesis 3:1.

When Satan spoke to Eve, He put a question mark where God had put a full stop! Satan will use the same tactic on us. Satan will try to put doubts into our minds. He will try to make us think that we are missing out on a lot of great things in life if we by follow God's plan for us.

In Genesis 2, we read that there were all kinds of fruit trees in the Garden of Eden but in the centre there were two trees. One was called the tree of life and the other the tree of the knowledge of good and evil. Adam and Eve were sinless at this time. God had instructed them as to what they could and could not do and warned them of the results of any disobedience to His instructions. God said:

"…You are free to eat from any tree in the garden; but you must not eat from the tree of the knowledge of good and evil, for when you eat of it you will surely die." Genesis 2:16-17.

Satan comes along to Eve and asks a subtle question. He had a two-fold intention:

- First, he wanted to put doubt into Eve's mind about the genuineness of God's instructions.
- Second, he wanted to confuse Eve as to which of the two trees God's instructions applied to.

Let us carefully examine what Satan said as many people seem to get this part of the story wrong. Satan said to Eve "Hey, did God really say "Do not eat from the tree of life"?" But God had not said "Do not eat from the tree of life." God's instruction to Adam mentioned only the tree of the knowledge of good and evil. Satan's question introduced both a doubt and a lie and his evil intentions succeeded. His question introduced doubt and confusion as to God's instruction to Adam and we suffer the consequences of the sin that followed Satan's conversation with Eve.

Do you know where you can recognise Satan today? I am sure that many churchgoers would immediately mention the nightclubs and the gambling casinos and I agree that Satan is definitely in those places. But Satan is also in churches and he is taking the Word of God and where God has put full stops, Satan is putting question marks. He is questioning the:

- Authority of the Word of God.
- Accuracy of the Word of God.
- Application of the Word of God.

There are churches where people do not believe the Bible is the Word of God. We hear frequently that some church dignitary has announced that the Bible contains myths and cannot be taken as literally true. Many churchgoers place the Bible in the same category as the Works of Shakespeare.

When the Bible speaks, God speaks. When Satan comes along with his question marks, he is doing what he did with Eve. Satan was saying to her: "Eve there is more to life. You are not getting everything out of life that there is! And God is such a killjoy. He has restricted you so much that you can never be the woman you ought to be! There is more to life, Eve!" That is what Satan will say to you. "You are missing out on all the fun of life!"

Take for instance sex. People out there who are not following God's standard for purity look at us and think we are a bunch of people who are sexually repressed, unhappy and dysfunctional. God says: "Sex is wonderful! Enjoy it in the confines of a marriage." But Satan comes along and says: "You are really missing out if you wait until marriage to have sex." Do you know what Satan says to married couples? "Hey, you are missing out if you refuse to go outside your marriage for a sexual partner!"

Satan has not changed his tactics one bit. Be careful you do not get into a *dangerous conversation* with the devil.

SECOND: THE DESTRUCTIVE CHOICE

Adam and Eve sin

"When the woman saw that the fruit of the tree was good for food and pleasing to the eye, and also desirable for gaining wisdom, she took some and she ate it. She also gave some to her husband who was with her, and he ate it. Then the eyes of both of them were opened, and they realised they were naked; so they sewed fig leaves together and made coverings for themselves." Genesis 3:6-7.

Now where did we get the idea this fruit was an apple? It was fruit that we are not familiar with from the tree of the knowledge of good and evil.

No matter how big those fig leaves were, they were not big enough, because they could never cover Adam and Eve's shame. This was lost innocence, the loss of purity. Because Adam and Eve, the father and mother of the human race, chose to sin, I want you to understand what that means to you and to me now, thousands of years later.

Adam and Eve planted in each one of us a seed, a tendency that we all have from birth. We all sin. Nobody had to teach you or me, or any other person to sin. It is part of our makeup. When Adam and Eve sinned, sin entered the human race.

Notice the steps Eve went through:

"When the woman *saw* the fruit of the tree was good for food, and pleasing to the eye, and also for gaining wisdom." Then, "she *took* some and *ate* it. She also *gave* some to her husband." Genesis 3:6.

These are the steps that many people take when they make a destructive choice and give in to sin. Like Eve they:

- See.
- Take.
- Use.
- Involve others.

These are usually the four steps that we take when temptation comes along and we fall into sin. Let me clarify one matter about sinful thoughts and temptation that I know causes problems. There is nothing wrong with the thought of a sin. Some Christians feel so dirty because sinful thoughts have entered their minds. They are not sins and may not be temptations. Thoughts come and go through your mind, you cannot help that. But when a thought begins to grab hold of you and you consider or fantasise about it, then it becomes a real temptation.

Billy Graham has a classic remark. He said: "You cannot keep the birds from flying over your head, but you can keep them from building a nest in your hair."

You cannot keep sinful thoughts from running through your mind but that is where you must deal with them if you want to avoid the temptations that will follow if you do not.

The First Step

It was when Eve saw the fruit that she began to think about it. Do you know what happens to a thought that you mull around in your mind? It can become a temptation. Eve's temptation became an act, because she took it.

The Second Step

Note that that Eve misunderstood God's requirement. Eve told Satan that God had said:

"You must not eat fruit from the tree that is in the middle of the garden, and you must not touch it, or you will die." Genesis 3:3.

Wait a minute. God did not say anything about *"touching"*. God only said: "Do not *eat* it!" People have always had a tendency to add to God's requirements with the result that they have made life more difficult for themselves. But Eve had it in her mind: "Hey, if I even touch it, I will have blown it!" So she saw it and then took it. Do you know what Satan placed in her mind? That she had reached the point of no return! He might as well have said to Eve, "You have already gone so far, you might as well go all the way!"

When Eve took the fruit, she had not sinned. When you think something and it becomes a temptation and you handle it, it is still not yet a sin.

The Third Step

Then she sinned. She ate the fruit. It became a part of her.

The Fourth Step

The sinner becomes the seducer. Eve offered the fruit to Adam. Adam had a choice. Did he obey the instruction God had given him or did he join his wife in her disobedience. Adam chose to join his wife.

Sin will get you in a lot of personal and spiritual trouble. Satan is as crafty and as devious as he has been from the beginning. He usually starts to drag you down with one little bitty sin and then tries to entice you to do more serious sins. Are there little bitty sins that do not matter to God? No, all sin is sin. But Satan would have you believe that there are some small sins that will have no bad consequences. Believe me, my many years as a Christian, and the experience I gained as a pastor, have taught me that sin will always have bad consequences. Because he is subtle, Satan will initially tempt us with things that we think are not going to harm us spiritually. But how long will it be before we get the taste for sin? That is what Satan wants to give us! Eve made a destructive choice.

God gives us all a choice. He does not force us.

THIRD: THE DIVINE CONFRONTATION

God confronts Adam and Eve about their sin

"Then the man and his wife heard the sound of the Lord God as he was walking in the garden in the cool of the day, and they hid from the Lord God among the trees of the garden. But the Lord God called to the man, 'Where are you?' He answered, 'I heard you in the garden, and I was afraid because I was naked; so I hid.'" Genesis 3:8-13.

God already knew the answers to all the questions that He asked. He was not saying, "Where are you" so that He could find them. They were not playing hide-and-seek. He knew where they were. He wanted them to admit that they were hiding from Him. If you are lost you phone for help. The first question you will be asked is: *"Where are you?"* To get to you where you should be, you need to know where you are. That is what God was asking of this couple.

"And He said, 'Who told you that you were naked? Have you eaten from the tree that I commanded you not to eat from?' The man said, 'The woman you put here with me—she gave me some fruit from the tree, and I ate it.' Then the Lord God said to the woman, 'What is this you have done?' The woman said, 'The serpent deceived me, and I ate.'" Genesis 3:11-13.

Have you ever noticed how much we all shift blame? It is never our fault. It is always somebody else's fault:

God came to Adam and said: "What have you done?"
Adam said, "It is not my fault. It is the woman's fault."
God came to Eve and said: "What have you done?"
Eve said, "It is not my fault. It is the snake's fault."
The poor snake did not have a leg to stand on.

One way we know for sure that they had fallen into sin was that they fell into "the shame game," which all of us have played. But God came looking for them. What a beautiful picture of our God. He is not a God who hides on the other side of the Universe saying, "Find Me if you can". He comes looking for us. Here is a question that I want you to answer. *Where are you trying to hide from God?*

Consider the sad picture. The Creator, the Lord God of the Universe who created all of the trees, who created the ground, who created the mountains, who created Adam and Eve, came walking in the garden and they think they can hide from Him! They are hiding behind some little trees! What were they thinking? *If I cannot see Him He cannot see me.* I am sure that we both agree that their attempt to hide from God was ridiculous. But it is no more ridiculous than the picture we have today of lots of people who are hiding behind their own trees. What are these present-day trees that so many feel the need to hide behind?

I have seen people hide behind:

- The tree of *self-righteousness*

    You can hear them saying, "I am a pretty good person. I am better than a lot of the people at that church." They are hiding behind the tree of self-righteousness and they think that God cannot find them.

- The tree of *riches*

    When God comes and looks for these people do you know what they do? They hold their chequebook out from behind the tree and say. "God you can have my money but you cannot have me. Leave me alone."

- The tree of *religion*.

    These people just follow some ritualistic pattern that gives their lives some structure. They do not have a personal relationship with God.

Do not be so quick to laugh at Adam and Eve who were hiding behind those trees in the Garden of Eden, when many people today hide behind trees that they have planted themselves.

FOURTH: THE DETAILED CONDEMNATION

God's punishment for disobedience

Before we think about this matter and before you judge that God is too harsh, consider what God had said: "The entire garden is yours. Enjoy it! But there is a boundary around one area. That area is My Holiness, which I reserve for Myself. Do not cross the boundary line! If you cross that line, you will be punished."

God is not capricious. He does not punish without prior warning. God always gives us a multitude of good choices. God says the same to you today, He says: "There are boundaries. There are lines. Do not you cross over them! I warn you. If you cross over the line, there is punishment, there are consequences."

Consequences and punishment

"So the Lord God said to the serpent, 'Because you have done this, cursed are you above all the livestock and all the wild animals! [Up until this time, a serpent did not crawl on his belly] You will crawl on your belly and you will eat dust all the days of your life. And I will put enmity between you and the woman, and between your offspring and hers; he will crush your head, and you will strike his heel.' To the woman he said, I will greatly increase your pains in childbearing; with pain you will give birth to children. Your desire will be for your husband, and he will rule over you. To Adam he said, 'Because you listened to your wife and ate from the tree about which I commanded you, 'You must not eat of it,' 'Cursed is the ground because of you; through painful toil you will eat of it all the days of your life. It will produce thorns and thistles for you, and you will eat the plants of the field. By the sweat of your brow you will eat your food until you return to the ground, since from it you were taken; for dust you are and to dust you will return." Genesis 3:14-19.

God spoke to the serpent first and then to Eve. God spoke to Adam last. They heard their punishment in the order that they had sinned.

The serpent:

God said to the serpent, "You are going to become a snake". Every time you see a snake today, it is a reminder, an object lesson of how sin will put you lower than anything else. When you see a snake slithering on its belly down in the dirt and the dust, you remember that sin will reduce all of us to the dust and to the dirt. I heard someone say about sin:

- It will take you farther than you ever wanted to go.
- It will keep you longer than you ever wanted to stay.
- It will cost you more than you ever wanted to pay.

How very true those words are. Every time you see a snake it is a reminder of the first sin.

But there is good news. Genesis 3:15 contains "the proto-evangelium" or "the pre-evangelism." We have the first reference to Jesus in the Bible. So where in this verse is Jesus mentioned?

God is saying to Satan:

"Satan you are going to have offspring.
The woman is also going to have offspring.
I am going to put conflict between them.
One day, Satan, He is going to crush your head.
You will bruise His heel."

As you read verse 15, you suddenly realise that God has used the words "He" and "His". Whose heel is God referring to? It is the heel of the Offspring of the woman. Who is "the Offspring of woman" that God is talking about? We know that the answer is Jesus because Galatians says:

"But when the time had fully come, God sent his Son, born of a woman..." Galatians 4:4

Verse 15 also tells us that God has only ever recognised two families on the face of this Earth. Did you realise that this is what God said to Satan after sin came into God's perfect world? Forget all this nonsense about the brotherhood of man and the fatherhood of God over everybody in the world. These are lies that have come from Satan's hell. Let me show you that Jesus also confirmed that there are only two families in this world. Jesus said to the Jewish religious leaders:

You are of your father the devil and the works of your father you are doing. John 8:44

Did you realise that there has always been conflict between religion and Christianity? Religious people were used by Satan to bruise the heel of the Messiah. When they nailed Jesus to the cross they put a nail through each foot. Did you know that was a fulfilment of Genesis 3:15? That was Satan, the snake, bruising the heel of the Offspring of the woman. When Jesus hung on the cross He said:

"It is finished." John 19:30.

Do you know what Jesus was doing when He was crucified? He was crushing Satan's head! Jesus' death was a total and complete victory over Satan and everything evil that is associated with him. God's words to Satan in Genesis 3:15 were proved to be true at the cross. A heel wound is not fatal but a head wound is. Because Jesus crushed Satan's head when He died on the cross, it means that you and I can stamp on Satan all we want to! How do we know this?

Paul wrote to the Christians at Rome:

"The God of Peace will soon crush Satan under your feet." Romans 16:20.

After speaking to Satan, God spoke to Eve.

Eve:

The FIRST condemnation

This concerned childbirth. God said that each time a woman brings a child into the world, it will be a life-threatening and painful experience. It is a reminder that sin always brings pain and suffering into this world.

The SECOND condemnation

This concerned her husband:

"Your desire will be for your husband and he will rule over you." Genesis 3:16.

The Hebrew word for 'desire' comes with the idea of 'legs'. This does not mean that a wife will spend her life running after her husband. Although she may if he does not tidy things away! No! It speaks of a hunger for approval. After sin came into the world, a perverse element entered the relationship between a man and a woman. Tension came into the relationship that was not there before. Some might say: "Well I think women have had a raw deal. This is a cruel punishment." We will come back to this later.

Adam:

God said to Adam: "The environment will be hostile to you. No longer can you just go out and pick fruit from the trees. You are going to have to work to support yourself and your family. There are going to be thorns, brambles and bushes. You are going to have to work and through blood, sweat and tears you are going to have to earn a living by the sweat of your brow." That is just part of what happened because of sin. Man is reduced to unending toil, constantly in the rat race. Work is not the curse given to men, drudgery is.

The death sentence:

God had said:

"...you must not eat from the tree of the knowledge of good and evil, for when you eat of it you will surely die." Genesis 2:17.

Adam and Eve already knew what would happen if they chose to sin. Their bodies would immediately be subject to death, a death sentence they have passed on to all of us. Death is always lurking at life's boundaries giving a sense of futility to whatever we do. A young man once said that his uncle had died a millionaire. A friend said: "No he did not. Who has his money now?"

We have read God's punishment for women and men. Sin has resulted in death for both sexes and whilst we live, suffering and subjection for women and drudgery for men. What I want you to note is this. These things were never intended to be punishment. God gives us the ability to counteract the consequences of those first sins:

- We help relieve the pain for women.
- We help the gardener in his struggles.
- We supply a computer for the office worker.
- We supply helpful appliances in the home.

What are all these devices designed to do? They alleviate the pains and struggles of life. Whenever we need to counteract the consequences of those first sins, God is reminding us of a very important truth. We are accountable to God. There are many who suppress or ignore this truth. They glibly think or say: "I am the

Captain of my fate, the Master of my soul," but we are constantly reminded that this is not true. We have limits to what we can do and the final limit is death. Because God imposes these consequences upon us, we are reduced to seeing ourselves as we really are. We are just dust. We are limited in what we can do and we desperately need God's help in our lives.

So remember, these consequences are not punishments but lessons that God wants to teach us.

"Adam named his wife Eve, because she would become the mother of all the living. The Lord God made garments of skin for Adam and his wife and clothed them." Genesis 3:20-21.

In that verse is a beautiful picture of blood atonement. Adam and Eve were trying to cover themselves with fig leaf clothes. I can imagine that when Eve put her fig leaf dress on Adam said: "Darling, you look stunning! I mean green is your colour!" But when God looked at their efforts to cover themselves, He said: "You can never cover your shame with the works of your own hands. I am the only One who can cover up your shame."

So God took skins. A skin comes from a living animal. The Bible does not say it but I will not be a bit surprised when I get to Heaven if we find out that it was a lamb, an innocent lamb that God killed to cover Adam and Eve. Throughout the Bible there was a lamb whose blood was shed to cover the shame and the sin of the human race. When Jesus died on the cross, He was our Lamb and His blood covers us, forgives us and cleanses our sins.

'Take and eat' were words of damnation for Adam and Eve. There came a Saviour who turned these words into words of Salvation.

"Jesus took bread, gave thanks and broke it and and gave it to his disciples saying 'Take it, this is my body.'" Mark 14:22.

There is nothing that we can do to purge the world of sin but we can repent of our personal sin and accept the Salvation that Jesus freely offers us.

Chapter 12 John 21:1-19

Do You Love Me?

Stephen Pile wrote the Harmondsworth: Penguin book-*The Return Of Heroic Failures*. I just love this story that he tells: "A trail-blazing burglar broke into a vast mansion on millionaires' row in June 1982 at Bel Air, Los Angeles. While on a sack-filling tour of this palatial structure, he went through the ballroom into the hall, down the escalators to the single-lane swimming arbour, up to the library across the dining-room, out of the annexe and into the conservatory containing sixty-three varieties of tropical plants and a cage full of sulphur-crested parrots. Deciding that now was the time to make a quick exit, he went back through the dining room, up to the gymnasium across the indoor tennis-court, down a spiral staircase to an enclosed patio with synchronised fountains, out of the cocktail lounge through junior's sound-proof drum studio and back into the roomful of increasingly excited parrots who normally see nobody from one day to the next. Panicking slightly, he ran back towards the library, through swing doors into a gallery containing the early works of Jackson Pollock, out through the kitchen across a jacuzzi enclosure and up two flights of stairs, at which point he became hysterical, ran outside along the balcony around the circular corridors, up more stairs, down the landing into the master bedroom and woke up the owners to ask them how to get out. In order to spare him further distress they arranged for a local policeman to escort him from the premises."

Stephen Pile's books were a success because we can all relate to failure. And if there is one way that human beings consistently underestimate God's love, it is perhaps in His loving longing to forgive. Our gracious God is the God of the "second chances". He wants to forgive us and help us learn from our mistakes. He yearns to help us to start again, from the beginning and "get back into the game."

If I had to pick anyone in the Bible as proof of this wonderful truth, it would be the Apostle Peter because he fouled up miserably over and over again. And each time Jesus forgave him and gave him another shot.

Dr. Warren Bennis wrote about a promising junior executive at IBM who was involved in a risky venture for the company and ended up losing ten million dollars. He was called into the office of Tom Watson Senior, the founder and leader of IBM for forty years and a business legend. The junior executive, overwhelmed with guilt and fear, blurted out: "I guess you have called me in for my resignation. Here it is. I resign." Watson replied: "You must be joking. I just invested ten million dollars educating you; I cannot afford your resignation."

Because of his repeated mess-ups, Peter might have had several conversations just like this with Jesus. Let us look at three well known examples.

FIRST: Matthew 14 tells us about that time on the Sea of Galilee, when in the midst of a storm Jesus came walking on the water toward the boat His disciples were in. Peter got out of the boat and began walking on the water toward Jesus. Peter took His eyes off Jesus and was overwhelmed by fear and doubt and would have drowned if Jesus had not saved him. Jesus referred to Peter as a man of little faith. When they got in the boat I can imagine that Peter said: "You are right about me, Jesus. I am big on dramatic gestures but low on faith and trust. I am full of questions and fears. It does not take much of a storm to stop me. Here is my resignation." And I think Jesus would have said: "You must be joking, Peter. I have just invested a miracle in you. I cannot afford your resignation."

SECOND: Matthew 16 tells us about the time when Peter made his famous confession that Jesus was the Messiah, the Son of the living God. Jesus said: "God told you this

Peter!" Not long after that event Jesus told His disciples that it was necessary for Him to go to the cross and when He said this, Peter pulled Him aside and began to rebuke Him in essence saying: "Jesus, do not talk like that!" Jesus responded by saying that Peter was speaking for Satan, that he was playing on the wrong team. Well, I can imagine Peter said: "You are right about me Jesus. I speak impulsively; I am always putting my foot in my mouth. Here is my resignation." And then Jesus said to Peter: "You must be joking Peter. I have just invested a revelation in you. I cannot afford your resignation."

THIRD: The best example we can consider was at the great crisis moment of Jesus' life. Peter had vowed: "I will follow you no matter how much it costs, Jesus, no matter what everybody else does." He could not keep that pledge for even a few hours and ended up denying Jesus three times. After Jesus' resurrection He appeared to Peter privately and when He did I can imagine that Peter said to Him: "You were right about me all along, Jesus. I totally failed You at Your point of greatest need. I denied and abandoned You. Here is my resignation." And Jesus would have said: "You must be joking Peter. I have just invested a resurrection in you. I cannot afford your resignation."

All this brings us to our passage of Scripture. I think it shows Jesus' patience and the gracious forgiveness and guidance that He once again gave to Peter to help him recover from a time of terrible failure and to get him back into the game. I want us to study it because all of us are like Peter. We all foul up and sin. We fail miserably and I believe Peter's experience can teach us the things we need to do to start all over again. Let us look at John 21:1-19.

"Afterward Jesus appeared again to his disciples, by the Sea of Tiberias. It happened this way: Simon Peter, Thomas (called

Didymus), Nathanael from Cana in Galilee, the sons of Zebedee, and two other disciples were together. "I'm going out to fish," Simon Peter told them, and they said, "We'll go with you." So they went out and got into the boat, but that night they caught nothing. Early in the morning, Jesus stood on the shore, but the disciples did not realise that it was Jesus. He called out to them, "Friends, haven't you any fish?" "No," they answered. He said, "Throw your net on the right side of the boat and you will find some." When they did, they were unable to haul the net in because of the large number of fish. Then the disciple whom Jesus loved said to Peter, "It is the Lord!" As soon as Simon Peter heard him say, "It is the Lord," he wrapped his outer garment around him (for he had taken it off) and jumped into the water. The other disciples followed in the boat, towing the net full of fish, for they were not far from shore, about a hundred yards. When they landed, they saw a fire of burning coals there with fish on it, and some bread. Jesus said to them, "Bring some of the fish you have just caught." Simon Peter climbed aboard and dragged the net ashore. It was full of large fish, 153, but even with so many the net was not torn. Jesus said to them, "Come and have breakfast." None of the disciples dared ask him, "Who are you?" They knew it was the Lord. Jesus came, took the bread and gave it to them, and did the same with the fish. This was now the third time Jesus appeared to his disciples after he was raised from the dead. When they had finished eating, Jesus said to Simon Peter, "Simon son of John, do you truly love me more than these?" "Yes, Lord," he said, "you know that I love you." Jesus said, "Feed my lambs." Again Jesus said, "Simon son of John, do you truly love me?" He answered, "Yes, Lord, you know that I love you." Jesus said, "Take care of my sheep." The third time he said to him, "Simon son of John, do you love me?" Peter was hurt because Jesus asked him the third time, "Do you love me?" He said, "Lord, you know all things; you know that I love you." Jesus said, "Feed my sheep. I tell you the truth, when you were younger you dressed yourself and went where you wanted; but when you are old you will stretch out your hands, and someone else will dress you and lead you where you do not want to go." Jesus said this to indicate the kind of death by which Peter would glorify God. Then he said to him, "Follow me!"" John 21:1-19.

Let us go back a bit so we can better understand all that went on that day by the Sea of Galilee:

- John's Gospel tells us that after Jesus rose from the dead He appeared to the disciples as a group twice.
- Matthew's Gospel tells us that the second time Jesus met with them, He told them to go to Galilee and wait there for Him.
- The disciples obeyed and made the journey up from Jerusalem and began to wait for Jesus to appear.

The days after the resurrection must have been a confusing time for the disciples. I mean they were excited and awed that Jesus was alive but they still felt as though they were in limbo. Jesus had appeared to them but only briefly and then He disappeared. They never knew when they might see Him next. He came and went without explanation or announcement. Well, this left the disciples with an uncertain and perplexed feeling. Plus, they were restless because nothing seemed settled. They did not know what was supposed to happen next. So, everything was still up in the air for them that day in Galilee.

Jesus had told them *where* to meet Him but not *when*. So they waited and waited hours, probably even days, with no sign of Jesus. And I think Jesus did this to teach His disciples that they must learn patience. After all, if they were going to be used to further His Kingdom, they would have to learn to wait on His timing and trust His eternal perspective. And, we must learn this discipline as well because when we grow impatient with waiting and take matters in our own hands, we always get into trouble. Waiting is the hardest work of faith but it is worth it.

Isaiah promised that there is a blessing for those who trust God's timing. He said:

"Since ancient times no no-one has heard, no ear has perceived, no eye has seen any God besides you, who acts on behalf of *those who wait for him*." Isaiah 64:4.

In Chapter 2 we looked at Abraham who had to trust God's promises to him for 25 years. Impatient Peter had not yet learned to trust God's timing so he said to the others: "I cannot sit around any longer. I have got to do something. Let us go fishing." They got a boat and spent the night trying to catch fish on the Sea of Galilee, which is the way professionals like Peter, John, James and Andrew did it back then. They would use torches to attract the fish and then snare them in their nets. Maybe they were not just killing time. I think they were also hoping to make some cash, something they would have been short on since Judas had absconded with their money.

They laboured all night but to no avail. I imagine they tried every trick in the book on every known fishing hole in the lake and were exhausted and exasperated because nothing worked. In my mind's eye other boats that were out that night had no trouble catching fish but to Peter and the others it seemed as if the fish avoided their nets on purpose. And I think that the fish did not come near the disciples' boat because they had been ordered not to. Perhaps Jesus commanded the fish to stay away to teach the disciples another lesson and to give them an experience that they could look back on and be reminded that as He said in John 15:

"Apart from me you can do nothing." John 15:5.

So that night of failure was not without its spiritual lessons and potential benefits. Spiritually we can do worse than fail. You see, we can succeed and be proud of our success. We can succeed and forget the One who gives or withholds. Failure can teach us how much we need God. It can remind us that any success we have is because He is the source of:

> "every good and perfect gift." James 1:17.

If we are not careful we praise ourselves for our successes. Maybe the disciples needed a night of unsuccessful fishing to remind them of their need for Jesus! About 6 am they gave up and began heading back to shore. When they were about 100 yards from the shore they heard a Voice calling out to them through the early morning mist. It was a Voice that they had heard before but did not quite recognise at first. The Voice said: "Friends, have you caught anything?"

The question had a little sting to it. No fisherman worth his bait wants to be reminded of failure! An amazing thing happened. They were honest in their reply. Fishermen actually admitted they had not caught anything! They did not even comment on the one that got away. So the Voice replied: "Well, try again. Put your net down on the right side of the boat. Do not quit yet. Give it another try." And they did and when they pulled the net in it was full of fish, so full in fact that they could not lift it into the boat. Their catch was indeed a miracle because the same fish, which had been ordered to stay away, were now ordered to be caught. I imagine that every fish in the lake clamoured to get in the disciples' nets that morning! And they did so because unlike men, fish always obey their Master!

At this point John, who tended to understand what was happening more quickly than Peter, recognised the Speaker and said: "It is the Lord!" Peter, who tended to act more quickly than John, wrapped his coat around himself, leapt into the sea and swam ashore. Does this seem backwards to you? Put on clothes and then jump in the water? It was not. The Jews regarded a greeting as a religious act that could only be done when one was clothed. So, even in his impulsiveness, Peter had enough of his wits about him to prepare himself to greet the Lord.

I can understand Peter's eagerness because something like this had happened three years earlier. Remember? After another night of fishing, with no fish to show for it, Jesus had asked Peter and his partners to row out a little deeper. They did so and caught so much fish that their boats began to sink. It was that first "fishing miracle" that led to Peter's call to follow Jesus and fish for men. So perhaps with this memory in his mind Peter, who was not patient enough to wait for the heavily laden boat to take him to shore, jumped in and swam.

When the disciples caught up with Peter they discovered that Jesus had already started making a breakfast of grilled fish and bread. Jesus asked them to bring some of the fish they had caught to augment the meal and then encouraged them to eat but no one wanted to go first. They just stood there. To me, as I read the way John writes about this incident, it seems as if the disciples were hesitant to approach Jesus. I can understand how they might have felt because as we read earlier, things had changed. I mean they were eager to see Jesus again but they were awed by Him. He was the same but He was also different. They loved Him but they could no longer be familiar with Him. These were not the old days.

Before Jesus died and rose again, the disciples had been more aware of His humanity than of His deity. Now they were more conscious of His deity. So they were awkward and hesitant at first. Verse 13 says that to break the ice

Jesus took the bread and the fish and put it in their hands and urged them to eat and they did so. The more they ate the more they talked, just like some of our church socials. And soon it was just like old times. It was a wonderful morning of fellowship with Jesus that they would never forget. After the meal, the other disciples must have gone back to the boat to clean the fish and to stow the gear.

This gave Jesus an opportunity to talk to Peter alone. In the conversation that ensued we see three steps that Peter had to take to start again:

- Confession.
- Contrition.
- Commitment.

They are the same steps that God guides us through so that we can receive the "second chances" that He so graciously offers us.

THE FIRST STEP: CONFESSION

As Jesus and Peter began to talk, Jesus did not reprove or condemn Peter for his failure on the night of His arrest. Jesus did not ask Peter:

- Are you sorry for what you have done?
- Do you promise never to fail Me again?
- Will you promise to try harder?"

Instead, Jesus probed Peter's heart three times to discover the depth of his love. I want to point out that Jesus did not refer to him by the nickname Peter that He had given to him that memorable day in the hills of Caesarea Philippi. Jesus simply called him: "Simon, son of John." And I think Jesus did this as if to say: "I will not presume that you want our old intimate relationship back. I will not presume you still want to wear the name Peter that I gave you. I will not presume on your love for me, Simon. Just tell me Simon, do you love me?"

Why did Jesus start at this point? Why was it so important for Peter to confess his love for Jesus in order for him to start all over again? The reason is simple when we realise that:

- Sin is not just breaking the commandments of God.
- Sin is breaking the heart of God.

Sin, by its very nature is not only against law but against love. Think about it. When a man cheats on his wife, what is the first thing she wonders "If he loves me, why did he do it?" When our children no longer respect us it breaks our hearts and we think about their behaviour and wonder if they still love us. It is the same with God. Jesus said:

"If you love me, you will obey what I command." John 14:15.

If we are to recover and start again, we must:

- Acknowledge our sin.
- Acknowledge our love for God.

Our love for God must be greater than our love for the pleasures of sin. You see, the truth is that if we love Jesus we will not betray Him. We will not disobey Him. Our love will be the motivation for our obedience. If we really love God, if God is truly first in our lives, we will only do things that please Him. It is only when our love of self rises to the top that we get into trouble.

Another thing, if we truly love someone we will care about

the things that they do. This is why Jesus said to Peter: "Do you love Me? Then care for My sheep." Jesus cares about people and this was seen so clearly during His earthly ministry. I mean, even though He was Holy God, He showed a passion for all people, even those who had failed and fouled up most in life, like the dishonest tax collectors, prostitutes and the social outcasts.

Jesus was repeatedly moved with compassion for people like you and me, even to tears, because He loved people. When He died on the cross He was not dying for a political cause or for some stubborn personal agenda. No, He willingly died for people. As Romans 5 says, our Lord demonstrated His love for us in this:

"While we were still sinners, Christ died for us." Romans 5:8.

With Jesus in a very real sense, it is: "Love Me and love My people." If we want to express our love for Jesus, we will spend our time loving others.

THE SECOND STEP: CONTRITION

A love for Christ is essential but it is not sufficient. For us to even want to start again, there must also be deep sorrow for our sin. King David learned this lesson through his own sinful failures. In Psalm 51 he prayed:

"You do not delight in sacrifice or I would bring it; you do not take pleasure in burnt offerings. The sacrifices of God are a broken spirit; a broken and contrite heart, O God, you will not despise." Psalm 51:16-17.

Only those who truly grieve over their sins will leave their sins and return to God! The road back to fellowship and service is always drenched with tears. I think Jesus set things up the way He did to help Peter:

- Remember and re-live what he had done wrong.
- Realise the seriousness of his actions.

I do not think it was a coincidence that:

- Jesus cooked fish on a charcoal fire. It would remind Peter of the charcoal fire that he sat around a few days earlier when he claimed he did not know Jesus.
- Jesus asked Peter three times if he loved Him. It was a reminder that Peter had denied Jesus three times.

Prior to the arrest of Jesus, Peter had boasted that his devotion to Jesus, his love for Him, was greater than that of the other disciples. In Matthew 26 Peter had said:

"Even if all fall away on account of you, I never will.... even if I have to die with you, I will never disown you."
Matthew 26:33-35.

But a few short hours later, when push came to shove, Peter denied Jesus three times. Do you remember the three things that Peter said that awful night?

- "I don't know what you're talking about..." Matthew 26:70.
- "I don't know the man..." Matthew 26:72.
- "I'm not His disciple." Matthew 26:74.

John 21:17 says that Peter was grieved the third time Jesus asked him about His love. He was grieved because he realised exactly what he had done that night. Peter felt pain for his sin. He had a broken and contrite heart. He knew that this was his biggest foul-up ever! I imagine Peter said to himself, "Some 'rock' I turned out to be! I have acted more like shifting grains of sand!" Jesus made

Peter re-live the events of that night to help him on the road to a new start because there can be no spiritual recovery without a sense of sorrow over sin.

To enable us to start again there must be CONFESSION of our sin and our love and deep CONTRITION over our wrong actions. But there is one more step on the road to a new start.

THE THIRD STEP: COMMITMENT

We must decide one again to live for Jesus, no matter what it costs us to do so. After Peter's confession of love, Jesus told him that a day would come when Peter would stretch forth his hands on a cross and another would fasten him and carry him to a place of execution, a place where he did not want to go. He would be crucified because of His commitment to Jesus. He told Peter this before He used those words that He had said to Peter three years earlier:

"Follow me." Matthew 4:19.

Jesus was saying: "Peter regardless of your past failures, I am still calling you to follow me. I am inviting you to serve me but it will be costly. If you accept, you will indeed fulfil your pledge to die for me." Peter accepted the "second chance" that Jesus offered him. He bravely renewed his commitment. In fact he was a changed man after that morning. Peter became strong, powerful and authoritative. He preached at Pentecost so boldly that 3,000 people put their faith in Jesus. Peter became one of the key leaders in the early church. He took seriously his new commitment to care for Jesus' sheep. The disciple who failed became the disciple who could be counted on because he put his faith in the God of the "second chances".

An old poem goes like this:

"I wish there was some wonderful place
Called the Land of begin again.
Where all our mistakes and all our heartaches
and all our poor selfish grief
Could be cast like a shabby old coat at the door
And never be put on again
I wish there was some wonderful place
Called the Land of begin again."

There is such a place. It is at the foot of the cross of Jesus. Peter began again and so can we. We can get up from our failures and go on to become all that God wants us to be.

This question of how we begin again came out of the heart of a person who had stumbled badly. He felt he had no right to pray and when he tried, he felt self-incrimination and condemnation.

We all deny our Lord in so many little ways but what do we do when the denial contradicts everything we have stood for and believed? We may ask:

❏ Is there a way back?
❏ How does the Lord deal with failures?

The answers that we need are vividly portrayed in the way Jesus dealt with Peter's denial. What was the reason Jesus asked and repeated three times this disarming and disturbing question? "Do you love me?"

The dialogue was not to prove once and for all to Peter that he had not loved Jesus and that he could not love Him adequately. The dialogue was to prove to Peter that despite all that had happened, Jesus still loved Peter and wanted his love.

Peter lived through some painful days of depression that he had brought on himself because He could not:

- Tell the Lord how he felt.
- Ask for forgiveness.
- Ask for a new beginning.

Remember, there had already been three post-resurrection opportunities for Peter to speak to Jesus, two in the upper room and one as he stumbled out of the sea that day at Galilee. Peter had totally missed the impact of the grace of God incarnate in Jesus. It is amazing to contemplate that the major thrust of Jesus' message was not that we ought to love God in our own strength but that God's love is freely given to us before we start. There is significance in the questions Jesus asked and Peter's responses.

The question that Jesus asked Peter, "Do you love me?" forced Peter to confess that he had not loved Jesus and probably could not love Jesus in his own strength. A cursory reading of the verses might cause you to wonder why Jesus repeated His question to Peter twice after Peter had already confirmed his love for Jesus in answer to His first question. You see, there were two words for love. Jesus chose to use the loftier word for love, a love of loyalty and commitment. Peter only responded with the inferior word for love. Peter's response was only an admission that: "You know, I am your friend." This was actually a confession of a lack of love of the quality that Jesus desired. Jesus repeated His question and once again using the loftier word for love. Jesus lovingly gave Peter a second opportunity to wash the dreadful memory of that night from his mind. Once again Peter said: "You know I am your friend." Then Jesus descended from the loftier word for love and asked if Peter was really his friend.

An aggrieved Peter confirmed for the third time only that: "You know, I am you friend." Peter persisted in his three-time repeated response, "You know I am your friend". He could not and did not use the loftier word for love that Jesus used, a love of loyalty and commitment. Let me ask you these questions:

- What would you think about the answer "I am your friend" in response to your question about how much you were loved?
- What would you think about the words "I am your friend" from someone who had failed you, even deserted and disowned you, in your time of need?

The reality was that Peter had not even been a friend to Jesus. He had failed at both loving and friendship. And Jesus had unreservedly given him both. What a contrast there now was from Peter's former over-confident attitude. No arrogance, no proud boasting and not even a glimmer of self-importance. He had reached his spiritual rock bottom. Peter is fully aware that Jesus knew all about him as is evident from his three answers. And yet, every time Jesus responded to him, Peter heard Jesus ask him to do something for Him. Jesus asked him to look after others. Jesus referred to these as, "My lambs" and "My Sheep."

And then, Peter heard Jesus tell him that he would be crucified one day and that his death would bring glory to God. Peter had boasted that he was willing to die for Jesus and now he knew that he would be crucified when he was old. He knew then that he had been forgiven. Jesus had never stopped loving him and He was still his friend. His cowardice, lying and cursing were in the past. Despite being told of his extremely painful death, Peter must have been delighted when he realised he now had a fresh start.

Once again he heard those words that required his commitment: "Follow Me."

Once Peter allowed the Lord to forgive him, we note that he forgave others who also failed even when other leaders of the early church refused to. Look at his relationship with John Mark. When this young failure defected from Paul's first mission, Paul refused to take him on further missions. Peter was one of those who were willing to let John Mark continue in God's service. Note that Peter affectionately refers to him as his son:

"She who is in Babylon, chosen together with you, sends you her greetings, and so does my son Mark." 1Peter 5:13.

Peter and John Mark are wonderful examples of the truths that we have been considering in this chapter.

What should we do when we have failed?

We begin again at the foot of the cross of Jesus. We must:

- Allow Him to give us back our sense of worth.
- Accept our status as His friend.
- Allow His friendship to capture our minds and emotions.

Then we must relax and allow Him to flash before the screen of our minds the kind of person He wants to enable us to be in our relationship with Him and our relationships with others. Peter was given a new image of himself as a leader and sensitive enabler of people. He became what the Lord sparked in his imagination. Later, at Pentecost, he received power to love the new life Jesus had pictured in his imagination. When the Living Christ returned in the power of the Holy Spirit at Pentecost and took up residence within Peter, this liberated Apostle became one of the bold leaders of the early church.

Will you let your thoughts be this? "Lord, you know what I have done with the gift of life. I know that I have failed you. But more than that, Lord, I know I love you. And that is all I need to know!"

Let Christ take up full residence in you. He is willing to forgive and release people like you and me. Is not that worth knowing? There is nothing better.

Chapter 13   Luke 1:5-25

How Can I Be Sure Of This?

In Luke 1-2, we learn about the miraculous birth of the Lord Jesus. However, there is *another* miraculous birth recorded in Luke Chapter 1, the birth of John the Baptist. Why did Luke include this when none of the other three Gospel writers even mention it? The answer is found on the last page of the Old Testament. In Malachi 4 we read:

"See, I will send you the prophet Elijah before that great and dreadful day of the Lord comes. He will turn the hearts of the fathers to their children, and the hearts of the children to their fathers." Malachi 4:5-6.

Four hundred years before Jesus was born, God gave the Old Testament Jewish Nation a final promise. He promised that the Messiah would come and He told them that before that happened, He would send Elijah as a forerunner. Then for 400 years God was silent.

Luke gives us a well thought out organised account of Jesus. He correctly saw the connection between the birth of John the Baptist and the coming of the forerunner, Elijah. He lets us know that after 400 years, God shattered the silence with the birth of John the Baptist. Remember those words from Malachi when you read them later in this passage from Luke 1: 5-25.

"In the time of Herod king of Judea there was a priest named Zechariah, who belonged to the priestly division of Abijah; his wife Elizabeth was also a descendant of Aaron. Both of them were upright in the sight of God, observing all the Lord's commandments and regulations blamelessly. But they had no children, because Elizabeth was barren; and they were both well on in years." Luke 1:5-7.

Zechariah and Elizabeth are the parents-to-be of John the Baptist. What do their names mean?

❑ Zechariah means "God remembers."
❑ Elizabeth means "God's oath," or "promise."

We learn later they lived simple lives out in the hills of Judea. They would have been considered unsophisticated by the elegant Jerusalem crowd but they were faithful servants of the Lord and both of them were descendants of Aaron. The one cloud that hung over their marriage was that they could not have children.

There are many of you who deal with the same problem that Zechariah and Elizabeth faced. You would love to have children but perhaps for a variety of reasons, you have not been able to. In Bible times there was a strong social stigma attached to women who were childless. They were called "barren" and many people interpreted it as some kind of punishment from God. Even that word *barren* meant shame for Elizabeth. It is a word that conjures images of a dry wind blowing across a lifeless desert. Zechariah and Elizabeth had prayed for a child for many years but now they were old and had probably stopped praying because they both thought that it was now impossible. Maybe they had forgotten that God specialises in the impossible.

Note something else about them. They were old folks, people we would call "forerunners". Maybe you think that you have entered spiritual retirement and that you have already done enough for God. Or perhaps you think that you have already received the greatest blessings that you will ever enjoy. Think again.

In this passage, we are going to see three steps that Zechariah took that allowed him to see God work in a miraculous way. You have probably heard of 12-step programmes for recovering addicts. We are going to look at the three steps you can take to see God work in your life. Do you want that? We are going to consider:

- Worship.
- Wonder.
- Willingness.

Then we are going to see that we can take the same steps that Zechariah took.

STEP 1: WORSHIP – the joy of meeting God

"Once when Zechariah's division was on duty and he was serving as priest before God, he was chosen by lot, according to the custom of the priesthood, to go into the temple of the Lord and burn incense. And when the time for the burning of incense came, all the assembled worshipers were praying outside. Then an angel of the Lord appeared to him, standing at the right side of the altar of incense. When Zechariah saw him, he was startled and was gripped with fear." Luke 1: 8-12.

In those days, there were thousands of priests, so the priestly duties had been divided up according to their priestly Order. When it came time for the Order of Abijah's division to perform the Temple duties, Zechariah went to Jerusalem. Most priests lived normal lives for most of the year but for two weeks during the year they were on duty. It was a time the priests anticipated all year long. There could have been hundreds of priests in the Order of Abijah, so each day they cast lots to see who would get to perform the special task of burning incense. One day, Zechariah was chosen for this very high privilege which he would have done either in the morning or in the evening.

This was such a high privilege that it could only be done by a priest once in a lifetime. It was a highly coveted task. One can only imagine the feelings Zechariah must have experienced the evening before his duty was due to be performed. On the one hand, he must have rejoiced in the high privilege that was his, which he had hoped for all his life. On the other hand, he must have reflected on Leviticus 10, which records the death of Nadab and Abihu, Aaron's sons, for carrying out this ritual in a wrong manner. The Bible says they offered "strange fire" and died as a result. Thus, there were the mixed feelings of rejoicing and fear. He probably carefully rehearsed in his mind exactly how he would perform his duty, so that he would emerge from the Most Holy Place alive.

While all the other priests remained outside the Temple building singing and praying, Zechariah entered the Most Holy Place. While the Temple complex was large, the actual Temple itself was rather small with only two rooms. Both rooms together were a little over 100 feet long and about 75 feet wide. The first room was the Most Holy Place. This was where the Altar of Incense was located. The Altar was just in front of the tall curtain that separated the Most Holy Place from the second room called the "Holy of Holies." Inside the Holy of Holies was the golden box called the Ark of the Covenant. The High Priest only entered this room on one day each year, the Day of Atonement. So, this was as close as Zechariah would ever get to where Jewish worshippers believed the Shekinah, the Glory of God, dwelt. You can imagine how much in awe he must have been.

It was Zechariah's job to ignite the incense that day. This was a mixture of spices and material that created a great deal of smoke and produced a pungent, sweet smell. The burning of incense had two important purposes:

- It was a picture of the prayers of God's people. Like the smoke of incense, our prayers waft upward into the presence of God. When the incense was lit inside the Most Holy place, the smoke would fill the room and begin to billow out from the openings around the top of the walls on either side of the room. As the other priests were outside praying, they would look for this smoke and it would be a picture of their prayers.
- It was also to veil God's awesome presence. On the Day of Atonement, this heavy smoke would veil the sight of the ark so the High Priest would not die from seeing God. When Moses first built the Tabernacle in the wilderness, Aaron made the initial sacrifice. God came and consumed the sacrifice with fire and smoke and from that time, the Jews were reminded of God's presence by the smoke of incense.

Even to this day, the Eastern Orthodox Church still use the burning of incense as part of their worship. When you visit the Church of the Holy Nativity in Bethlehem, the air inside the Church is often thick with the smoke of incense. The smoke assaults all your senses. You can:

- See it.
- Smell it.
- Taste it when you breathe.
- Feel it on your skin.
- Hear the fires sputtering inside the censers.

Although worship is not a sensory experience, when you have a real experience of worship, it transcends all your senses. The incense was to remind Jewish worshippers of this truth.

As Zechariah was performing his duty something amazing happened. The Angel Gabriel appeared to him and brought him a message from God. Zechariah reacted in the same way most people mentioned in the Bible do when they see an angel, he was terrified! Zechariah had a divine encounter. He became so aware of the power and presence of God that he was in awe. Now you have got to remember that for 400 years there had not been a single recorded incident of God delivering a message to Israel in any form. For thousands of days, priests had gone through the same religious motions but they had not had a revelation from God. You cannot say that old Zech was *expecting* this to happen. It was a first for him! This was an unexpected visitation from Heaven.

Let me ask you two questions. When you worship:

- What do you expect?
- What do you experience?

What is our personal experience of worship?

How many times have we simply gone through the motions? Do you recognise this pattern of behaviour?

- Walk in and sit down.
- Stand up, sing a little and sit down again.
- Pass the offering plate or bag.
- Open the Bible, listen.
- Stand up and sing again.
- Walk out.

If you recognise this scenario, is it not true that when we

follow this pattern, we never really meet God? And yet the primary purpose of worship is the joy of meeting God. Some might say: "I thought God was everywhere. How can you meet Him?" When we worship, we are focused on God and we become more aware of His presence with us. We will consider this again later in the chapter. WORSHIP is the first step in seeing God work.

STEP 2: WONDER – the joy of hearing from God

"But the angel said to him: 'Do not be afraid, Zechariah; your prayer has been heard. Your wife Elizabeth will bear you a son, and you are to give him the name John. He will be a joy and delight to you, and many will rejoice because of his birth, for he will be great in the sight of the Lord. He is never to take wine or other fermented drink, and he will be filled with the Holy Spirit even from birth." Luke 1:13-15.

One lady said she would not have minded keeping young John in the nursery! He certainly would not need the help of any supernanny or social worker.

"Many of the people of Israel will he bring back to the Lord their God. And he will go on before the Lord, in the spirit and power of Elijah." Luke 1:16-17.

Remember the last words of the Old Testament? Here is the connection:

"To turn the hearts of the fathers to their children and the disobedient to the wisdom of the righteous - to make ready a people prepared for the Lord." Luke 1:17.

Zechariah asked the angel, "How can I be sure of this? I am an old man and my wife is well on in years." The angel answered:

"I am Gabriel. I stand in the presence of God, and I have been sent to speak to you and to tell you this good news. And now you will be silent and not be able to speak until the day this happens, because you did not believe my words, which will come true at their proper time." Luke 1:19-20.

Wow! What a message! The first thing Gabriel said was:

"Do not be afraid." Luke 1:13.

By the way, this is the most common thing that angels say. Obviously, that is because most people are scared out of their wits when they see one! However, I have found that this is also one of the most common messages that God delivers to people when they worship Him. Maybe you tremble inside because you are afraid that something bad is going to happen. If you listen, God will whisper to you: "Do not be afraid, I am here. I will take care of you." Then you can say, like David:

"Even though I walk through the valley of the shadow of death, I will fear no evil, for you are with me." Psalm 23:4.

The next message Gabriel delivered is: "Your prayer has been heard." Now you may think Gabriel is talking about Zechariah's prayer for a child but I do not think so. By Zechariah's response, it is obvious he had given up on the idea. And remember Zechariah was in the Temple praying as a priest on behalf of the Nation of Israel. What was the Nation praying for? What had their prayer been for hundreds of years? They had been praying for the Messiah to come, for God's Kingdom to come.

Jewish worshippers are still praying for that today. God was going to answer the Nation's prayer and provide the child that Zechariah and Elizabeth had longed to have for so many years

Wow! What an awesome God He is. Then Gabriel gives proof that God has finally decided to break His silence by connecting the birth of John the Baptist with His promise given in Malachi. Gabriel tells Zechariah that his son will be the "Elijah" who would fulfil those final words of the Old Testament and prepare the Jewish Nation for the coming of their Messiah. God was answering Zechariah's prayer. The silence was broken.

Today, for some of you, it seems that God has been silent for a long time. When I mention the wonder and the joy of hearing from God you might be saying to yourself: "I have not heard from God for a long, long time." You may think that God is angry with you. Let me ask you. Are you experiencing the joy of hearing from God? It may be that God is speaking, but you are not listening. We will consider more about that later. For now, notice Zechariah's response to Gabriel. He said, "There are two reasons why what you say cannot happen."

- The first one is me. I am old.
- The second one is my wife. She is too old.

In the Greek he used the normal word for "old" when he referred to himself but when he described Elizabeth he used a phrase, which literally says: "Too many years have taken their toll on her." It is almost as if he was saying: "I am old, but the problem is really with my wife." Had Zechariah forgotten about:

- Sarah who was old and barren? She gave birth to Isaac.
- Hannah who was barren, yet gave birth to Samuel?

Sometimes we think that a miracle is something that only

happens to others.

Gabriel is not impressed with Zechariah. In fact, he is a little miffed. He said, "You do not believe me? You do not believe God? Unbelief can damage your health, friend. Okay, just to show you, you are not going to be able to talk until all of this has been fulfilled." I do not know what constitutes the greater miracle. An elderly woman having a baby or a preacher being quiet for nine months!

As we move from WORSHIP to WONDER and into the third step, let us stop here for a moment:

- Zechariah met God in WORSHIP. That was wonderful.
- Zechariah heard from God and that was amazing.

But now it is up to Zechariah. Is He going to do anything about what He has heard and experienced? He could have:

- Left the Temple, unable to talk and still doubting God.
- Chosen to do nothing about what Gabriel told him.

If he had, then Zechariah would have lived the rest of his life simply known as the priest who was struck dumb by God in the Temple. Millions of Christians gather in thousands of churches all across this globe every week:

- Some never get to the first step of worship.
- Others worship but they never hear God's voice.

But I am convinced that there are many who take the first two steps but then they leave and do nothing about what they have heard!

How sad.

STEP 3: WILLINGNESS – the joy of obeying God

"Meanwhile the people were waiting for Zechariah and wondering why he stayed so long in the temple. When he came out, he could not speak to them. They realised that he had seen a vision in the temple, for he kept making signs to them but remained unable to speak. When his time of service was completed, he returned home. After this his wife Elizabeth became pregnant and for five months remained in seclusion. 'The Lord has done this for me,' she said. 'In these days he has shown his favour and taken away my disgrace among the people.'" Luke 1: 21-22.

Zechariah came out of worship a changed man. Everyone knew he had met God, seen a vision. By the way, when you have truly been with God, other people can usually discern that. I like verse 23 that says:

> "When his time of service was completed he went home."
> Luke 1:23.

In other words, an encounter with God is no reason for us to shirk our basic responsibilities. Zechariah went home and if he and Elizabeth had previously given up on their attempts to have a baby, they resumed because one morning Elizabeth is a little nauseous and after a few weeks, she realises a miracle has happened. When she is certain, she said to Zechariah: "Guess what darling? I am pregnant." Do you know what Zechariah said? Nothing, because he cannot talk, remember?

Let me ask two questions.

Question 1. How many wives would like to live with a husband who could not speak for nine months? You say: "My husband does not say much more than 'What is there to eat?' anyway!"

Question 2. How many husbands would like to live with a wife who could not ...

Forget it. It is not going to happen!

The point I want you to see is very important. After WORSHIP and the WONDER of hearing from God, Zechariah demonstrated WILLINGNESS. He was willing to do his part in God's plan. Sure enough, Elizabeth is pregnant. She is so happy! She praises God for taking away her reproach among the people. Now, as an old woman she is expecting her first child. What a miracle! I have known couples that have tried and tried for a child for years. They visit doctors and take treatment and then, many times when it seems that it will never happen, they find themselves expecting a child. If that has happened to you, you know how Elizabeth felt.

Remember what the names of Zechariah and Elizabeth mean? In the birth of John the Baptist, their two names, "God remembers" and "His oath" were joined to form a message from God. God remembered His Oath.

Do you know what the name John means in Hebrew? God is gracious. God is gracious and He remembers His oath from Malachi 4.

Now that is a great story but what can we learn from it? I would like to assist you in conducting what I call a PERSONAL SPIRITUAL INVENTORY.

Take a moment and ask yourself these three questions:

Question One:

Am I often aware of God's presence in private and corporate worship?

Notice that there are two settings for worship.

- First, there is private worship. When you are alone with God, are you aware that He is there with you?
- Second, there is corporate worship. When people gather together to focus on God, are you aware of God's presence?

As much as I need and enjoy corporate worship, I need to meet God every day. I need to take time to focus on His presence, to read His Word and to worship Him. I sing to Him, I talk to Him. I have some glorious experiences of worship all alone. Do you? God is always present with us but when we focus exclusively on Him, He reveals Himself in a way that is different than at any other time. Like the song says, *"Sometimes it causes me to tremble, tremble."*

Some may be reading my words and say. "I agree. Worship is a private experience. That is why I do not believe you have to go to a church to worship. I can worship in the garden, on the golf course, or even in my own house." Of course you can. But you cannot escape the fact that the Bible commands us to gather together with other believers and worship the Lord together. The Psalmist says:

> "Glorify the Lord with me: let us exalt his name together."
> Psalm 34:3.

Hebrews 10:25 says that we are not to miss gathering together to encourage one another.

If you want to make the most of your corporate worship experience, make sure you have a dynamic personal worship time. If the only time you ever worship is when you are in a church gathering, your worship experience will be rather shallow. There is a verse I often use when I think of personal and corporate worship. It is in James 4:

"Come near to God and He will come near to you. Wash your hands, you sinners and purify your hearts, you double-minded." James 4:8.

When I am in a church building worshipping God, I try to forget that anyone else is there except Jesus. I try to visualise myself drawing near to God. In order to do that, I must first ask Him to cleanse me, to purify my heart.

Look at the words "double-minded." What does that mean? It is the reason some may attend a worship service but never truly worship. It is because we are not single-minded in our pursuit of meeting God.

Experience has taught me that many of our "worship problems" are self-inflicted. They present themselves when we have too much on our minds or we are thinking about the wrong things.

Do you recognise any of these problems, or ones that are similar, that have robbed you of your time of worship?

- You are cross because the church car park was full.
- You are cold because the boiler is faulty.
- You do not like the music or the choice of hymn.
- Someone else is sitting in your favourite seat.
- You are not the preacher's greatest fan.
- You cannot stop thinking about all you have to do later.

Whatever your problem, it will stop your heart from being pure in its desire to meet God. Worship involves clearing your mind of everything else except the glorious thought that God is here and I have to come to worship and adore Him.

That is single-minded worship.

Question Two.

Am I able to discern God's voice speaking to me?

This was the second step in Zechariah's experience. In today's frenzied world there are many voices clamouring for our attention, some legitimate and some not. Sometimes it is hard to know among so many which voice is God's voice. Is life for you like walking through the middle of a noisy fairground? Do people yell at you from all sides? Even those who do not work or live relatively quiet lives are bombarded with all sorts of messages, from people, and from the media. How can you learn to:

DISCERN God's voice?

This is not your problem because:

- He will make Himself clear to you.
- He is the Father and you are His child.
- It is His responsibility to let you know what He wants.

DISTINGUISH God's voice from all other voices?

We hear God's voice in:

- His Word. That is the main way God speaks to us. When you read your Bible or meditate on it, are you able to hear God's voice speaking to you? If the answer is "no," then it may be that you are not listening when God *is* speaking. Are you tuned in when you read and study the Word?

- Prayer dialogue. Notice the word "dialogue" because for many people, prayer is a monologue. You talk to God but you do not take time to listen to Him. Some people do not pray. They "say prayers." That is, they may repeat some words they have memorised and it is no different to reciting a poem to themselves. Prayer is a conversation. It is vital that we take the time to listen for God's "still, small voice" when we pray.
- Understanding your circumstances. If you do not hear God in the first two ways, it is unlikely that you will be able to understand what God is doing in the circumstances of your life. Someone said that God's Hand is in the glove of human circumstances and I have found this to be correct. God is usually trying to tell us something through events that happen around us but we must be seeking to interpret every event in the light of His Word.
- Godly advice from God's people. Jesus has a body today called the church. Sometimes when you seek counsel from godly people, God will speak to you through them. Incidentally, I do not believe in "unsolicited advice." Sometimes a person will say to you, "God told me to tell you something …" Be very wary. But when you humbly approach those whose wisdom you respect and ask them for advice, God can use them to help you to determine His will for you.

Remember, WORSHIP that does not lead to the WONDER of hearing from God is incomplete worship.

The third step still remains: WILLINGNESS.

Question Three.

Am I willing to obey God for the impossible?

God knows whether or not you are willing to obey. He did not force Zechariah to obey Him but I believe God knew that Zechariah had a willing heart. How? Zechariah was a faithful man. If you are faithful in the small things, God will entrust you with the big things. In Luke 6 Jesus says:

> "Why do you call me "Lord, Lord," and do not do what I say?" Luke 6:46.

Then Jesus described the life of a person who heard His Word but did not obey Him. I used to think this described a person who was totally alienated from God, a person who had never approached God and certainly one who had not heard from God. Actually this verse describes those who have taken the first two steps that we have just looked at. They have met Jesus and heard His Word. They just are not willing to obey Him. Jesus described their life:

> "But the one who hears my words and does not put them into practice is like a man who built a house on the ground without a foundation. The moment the torrent struck that house, it collapsed and its destruction was complete." Luke 6:49.

Pregnancy seemed totally impossible for Elizabeth, yet she and Zechariah obeyed God and then trusted God. There is a great principle of obedience that is woven into the fabric of God's Word and it is this. When you choose to obey God, He then gives you the power to obey Him.

What has God asked you to do that seems impossible? What about:

- ❏ Loving someone who is unloving to you?
- ❏ Forgiving someone who has hurt you deeply?
- ❏ Regarding all your income as belonging to God?
- ❏ Sharing your faith with your lost family and friends?

When God sees a willing heart in you, then He will provide you with the supernatural power to accomplish what He tells you to do.

Chapter 14   Psalm 22

Why Have You Forsaken Me?

When you travel through some countries, the landscape is cluttered with hundreds, probably thousands of small temples that house or are dedicated to manmade gods. In the evenings millions of people walk to these temples with their gifts and their sacrifices. They hope at some point to gain the favour of the gods. Why? They want deliverance from the hopelessness and despair in which they live. You also see Christian churches, easily identified by the cross on the building. It is the *cross* that:

- Distinguishes Christianity from every other religion of the world.
- Has made a fundamental difference to the whole of mankind.
- Takes us from hopelessness and despair to a life that is worth living.

We do not need to concern ourselves with sacrifices, gifts and offerings to gain the favour of the gods. We do not need to hope that somehow we can appease them and get their favour. This is because the cross represents the reality that:

- Our God sacrificed Himself
- God is the one who offers *us* the gift.

Those who place their trust in Jesus' death on the cross experience His salvation. It is the cross that takes us from hopelessness and despair to life. Of course, when we talk about the cross we understand that it is symbolic of God

Himself who became flesh and suffered and died on that cross in payment for your sin and mine. What it cost God to provide us with His free salvation, we will never know. The closest we have to understanding that is found in the Old Testament and is recorded in Psalm 22.

"My God, my God, why have you forsaken me? Why are you so far from saving me, so far from the words of my groaning? O my God, I cry out by day, but you do not answer, by night, and am not silent. Yet you are enthroned as the Holy One; you are the praise of Israel. In you our fathers put their trust; they trusted and you delivered them. They cried to you and were saved; in you they trusted and were not disappointed. But I am a worm and not a man, scorned by men and despised by the people. All who see me mock me; they hurl insults, shaking their heads: "He trusts in the LORD; let the LORD rescue him. Let him deliver him, since he delights in him." Yet you brought me out of the womb; you made me trust in you even at my mother's breast. From birth I was cast upon you; from my mother's womb you have been my God. Do not be far from me, for trouble is near and there is no one to help. Many bulls surround me; strong bulls of Bashan encircle me. Roaring lions tearing their prey open their mouths wide against me. I am poured out like water, and all my bones are out of joint. My heart has turned to wax; it has melted away within me. My strength is dried up like a potsherd, and my tongue sticks to the roof of my mouth; you lay me in the dust of death. Dogs have surrounded me; a band of evil men has encircled me, they have pierced my hands and my feet. I can count all my bones; people stare and gloat over me. They divide my garments among them and cast lots for my clothing. But you, O LORD, be not far off; O my Strength, come quickly to help me. Deliver my life from the sword, my precious life from the power of the dogs. Rescue me from the mouth of the lions; save me from the horns of the wild oxen. I will declare your name to my brothers; in the congregation I will praise you. You who fear the LORD, praise him! All you descendants of Jacob, honour him! Revere him, all you descendants of Israel! For he has not despised or disdained the suffering of the afflicted one; he has not hidden his face from him but has listened to his cry for help. From you comes the theme of my praise in the great assembly; before those who fear you will I fulfil my vows. The poor will eat and be satisfied; they who seek the LORD will praise him— may your hearts live forever! All the ends of the earth will remember and turn to the LORD, and all the families of the nations will bow down before him, for dominion belongs to the LORD and he rules over the nations. All the rich of the earth will feast and worship; all who go down to the dust will kneel before him—those who cannot keep themselves alive. Posterity will serve him; future generations will be told about the Lord. They will proclaim his righteousness to a people yet unborn —for he has done it." Psalm 22.

In this Psalm we read some of the words that were spoken by Jesus from the Cross. It is hard to imagine what Jesus must have thought about as He hung there on that cross some 2,000 years ago. I think sometimes that because we are so aware of His deity, the fact that He is God, we fail to recognise or appreciate His humanity. As Jesus hung on that cross, He was subject to the agonies, the emotions and the suffering of any human. What did He think about? How did He process His thoughts?

This Psalm is identified as a "Psalm of David" and it is a prophecy about Jesus and those hours when He hung on the cross. It may very well be that Jesus meditated on this Psalm as He was being crucified. We can identify thirty three specific prophecies concerning Jesus that were all specifically and perfectly fulfilled at the cross. That is an impressive number of prophesies when we realise that this Psalm was written a thousand years before Jesus was born. Ray Stedman has written a book on selected Psalms. I like the way he illustrates Psalm 22. He says:

"All the world knows that on November 22, 1963, President John Kennedy was assassinated in Dallas, Texas, while riding down a Dallas street in a motorcar. Suppose there had been in existence a document which predicted this event and which we knew to have been written in A.D. 963. That was about the time of the height of the Byzantine empire, when most of the Western World was ruled from Constantinople, much of Europe was only sparsely inhabited by barbarian tribes, and America was not yet discovered. Suppose that a document had been prepared in that ancient day which predicted that a time would come when a man of great prominence, head of a great nation, would be riding down a street of a large city in a metal chariot not drawn by horses, and would suddenly and violently die from the penetration of his brain by a little piece of metal hurled from a weapon made of wood and iron, aimed at him from the window of a tall building, and that his death would have world-wide effect and cause world-wide mourning. You can imagine with what awe such a document would be held today. Such a prediction would be similar to what we have in Psalm 22. That hypothetical prediction would have been made even before the invention of the motorcar, or of firearms, and five hundred years before the discovery of America. It would be regarded as fantastically accurate. Yet we have that very sort of thing in this psalm."

After Jesus had risen from the dead, He met two of His disciples who were walking to Emmaus. He explained to them that they should have known about His death, burial and resurrection because these events were prophesied:

- In the writings of Moses.
- In the Prophets.
- In the Psalms.

I believe that when Jesus mentioned the Psalms, He was referring to Psalm 22 that so clearly outlines the suffering, the agony and the anguish of crucifixion.

Before we look at the content of the Psalm itself, we learn something just from its structure. It was written in style that alternates between the anguish of the moment as Jesus suffered on the cross for sin and the thoughts that Jesus was having about God and God's person and character. It goes back and forth like that. These transitions are usually identified by the words "yet" or "but". For instance we read that:

- He endured His suffering,
  yet this is what He knew to be true... Verses 3 & 9.

- He endured His suffering,
  but this is what He knew to be true... Verse 19.

In this Psalm you will see the balance that will enable you to endure the difficult times in your life. The Christian is not exempt from the realities of life. But, unlike the unbeliever, the Christian also understands what is true about God as revealed in His Word. It is that balance that gets the Christian through the sufferings of life and that is certainly modelled in this Psalm.

The opening verse of Psalm 22 clearly identifies Jesus as the speaker. If you look at the Gospels, these are the words that come from the lips of Jesus as He was crucified:

"My God, my God, why have you forsaken me?" Psalm 22:1.

In a way that certainly cannot be humanly explained or understood, there was a separation between God the Father and God the Son. It was the first time in all eternity and it was the last time in all eternity that there was some level of break in Their fellowship. How grateful we should be that God never requires us to understand spiritual truths. God's blessings for us depend only on our belief and trust.

We do know that the Bible teaches from cover to cover that it is sin that separates us from God. When Jesus was crucified, He became the sin bearer. In fact, Jesus became more than the One who was bearing our sins. The Apostle Paul wrote that Jesus became:

"sin for us". 2 Corinthians 5:21.

When Jesus became "sin for us", it created a separation between God the Father and God the Son. Jesus feels the anguish of that and He cries out:

"Why have you forsaken me? Why are you so far from saving me, so far from the words of my groaning?" Psalm 22:1.

That word "groaning" is a dramatic Hebrew word. It was used to describe a lion's roar, claps of thunder and an animal that was crying out in distress. So it is a very vivid term that Jesus, in His anguish, cried out to the Father.

"O my God, I cry out by day, but you do not answer; by night, and am not silent." Psalm 22:2.

You remember what the Gospel writers tell us that from 12:00 noon to 3:00 in the afternoon, the land became dark as if it was night. Jesus' cry is probably a reference to that. Both in the light and in the darkness, while Jesus hung on the cross, He cried out but it seemed that God did not care, like God was not listening to Him and then He says:

"Yet you are enthroned as the Holy One". Psalm 22:3.

This is the alternate thought. Jesus remembers what is true about God and why the cross is necessary. It was about the holiness of God and the fact that God in His holiness could not have fellowship with sin. Therefore, that is the reason for this separation and Jesus is remembering that. He is remembering what is true:

"In you our fathers put their trust; they trusted and you delivered them. They cried to you and were saved; in you they trusted and were not disappointed." Psalm 22:4,5.

This is a familiar pattern in the Psalms generally. In the midst of suffering and anguish, we are encouraged to go back and review the faithfulness of God. Oftentimes in the midst of suffering it feels as though God has forsaken us, is not listening to us and does not care about us. And it is in those moments that we go back and repeat the faithfulness of God to His people generation after generation. This is what Jesus was doing at this point on the cross. Sometimes it is a long time after we have gone through difficulty or suffering that we are able to look back and see that God was being faithful to us all the time.

Jim Collins has written a book *'Good To Great'*. He talked with U.S. Admiral Jim Stockdale, who was a prisoner of war for eight years during the Vietnam War. He talked about how he survived. Stockdale says: "I never lost faith in the end of the story. I never doubted not only that I would get out but also that I would prevail in the end and turn the experience into the defining event of my life, which, in retrospect, I would not trade." Collins goes on and he writes: "I did not say anything for many minutes, and we continued the slow walk toward the faculty club, Stockdale limping and arc-swinging his stiff leg that had never fully recovered from repeated torture. Finally after about a hundred metres of silence, I asked, "Who did not make it out?" "Oh, that is easy," he said. "The optimists." "I do not understand," I said, now completely confused, given what he had said a hundred metres earlier. The optimists. They were the ones who said, 'We are going to be out by Christmas.' But Christmas would come and Christmas would go. Then they would say, 'We are going to be out by Easter.' But Easter would come, and Easter would go. And then Thanksgiving, and then it would be Christmas again. And they died of a broken heart." Another long pause and more walking. Then he turned to me and said, "This is a very important lesson. You must never confuse faith that you will prevail in the end—which you can never afford to lose—with the discipline to confront the most brutal facts of your current reality, whatever they might be."

That is a good lesson for us to learn. That is what Jesus was doing on the cross. He was thinking about the faithfulness of God and He knew where the story ended. But He still has to endure the brutal facts of the moment:

"I am a worm and not a man, scorned by men and despised by the people. All who see me mock me; they hurl insults, shaking their heads: 'He trusts in the LORD; let the LORD rescue him. Let him deliver him, since he delights in him.'" Psalm 22:6-8.

When you read the Gospels you realise that this section of the Psalm was perfectly fulfilled by the enemies of Jesus. This was exactly what they did and said at the cross. I suppose a sceptic could say that Jesus fulfilled the prophecies of Psalm 22 because He knew the Psalm and He recited His part. But how would a sceptic explain the fact that the enemies of Jesus perfectly fulfilled their part in word and deed? Did they read Psalm 22 and recite their part? Such a suggestion deserves to be ignored.

In verse 6, we read that as Jesus took our sin upon Himself, as He became the sin bearer, He said, "I am a worm." Some people think that this is a reference to a worm called the crimson crocus because when the worm was crushed it created a crimson dye. In Isaiah 53 we read:

"But he was pierced for our transgressions, he was crushed for our iniquities; the punishment that brought us peace was upon him, and by his wounds we are healed." Isaiah 53:5.

Jesus was crushed for our iniquities and in a sense He was crushed that we might be stained by His blood. Jesus endured all this that we might be forgiven. He was so despised, so rejected, so appallingly treated that He cried out that He was no longer a man, merely a worm.

We live in a culture where so many are constantly trying to establish the basis of their self-esteem and invariably trying to establish their self-esteem apart from God. Some say you basically just need to have good thoughts about yourself and that you need to think high esteem thoughts. Even though you may not be good, even though your thoughts do not live up to reality, they would encourage you to manufacture a sense of esteem. But that is really just a futile mental exercise. There is no substance to that. We do struggle with questions about ourselves:

- What is our value?
- What is our worth?

And we certainly do not want to be called a worm.

That is evident by the way we have re-written the hymnbook. The great old hymn says:

"Alas! and did my Saviour bleed, and did my Sovereign die? Would He devote that sacred Head for such a worm as I?"

We cannot take that. We are not worms, in our opinions. So we have re-written the hymn. If you look it up in the hymnbook it now says:

"Would He devote that sacred Head for such a sinner as I?"

We are sinners but we are not worms. But when Jesus hung on the cross and took our sin, He said, "I am a worm; I am not a man" and then He added:

"Yet You brought me out of the womb; you made me trust in you even at my mother's breast. From birth I was cast upon you; from my mother's womb you have been my God."
Psalm 22:9-10.

This is the alternate thought. Jesus is remembering what is true about God.

Jesus is feeling that:

- He is being forsaken.
- His cry is not being heard.
- He is a worm and not a man.
- He is despised and rejected.

Yet He remembers that this is part of the sovereign plan of the Father. God had guided and protected Him all the way through His life and brought Him to this moment on the cross. This is not a horrible mistake. This is the fulfilment of the will of the Father.

Jesus often said that He had come to do the will of the Father. And now in these moments He remembered that the cross was part of God's plan for Him. He was accomplishing the perfect will of the Father.

There had been occasions in His life when He had been protected from His enemies. A great example of that was when Jesus was an infant and Herod the King wanted Him dead. God intervened and spoke to Joseph and Joseph and Mary fled to Egypt with the infant Jesus so that His life might be spared.

Throughout His life, the Father guided Him and protected Him and brought Him to this moment on the cross. Now Jesus is rehearsing that.

"Do not be far from me, for trouble is near and there is no-one to help." Psalm 22:11.

Jesus begins to lay out pictures, metaphors, and images of

His enemies and His suffering in verses 12-18.

Jesus said about His enemies:

- They are like "the strong bulls of Bashan".

  Bashan was the name of the area we would call the Golan Heights. It was a very fertile and good area for livestock. Bashan bulls were strong and powerful. His enemies were like these powerful bulls.

- They "open their mouths wide against me". They were like lions wanting to devour Him.

Jesus said about His suffering:

- "I am poured out like water". He is melting away and is being poured out.
- "All my bones are out of joint". During crucifixion the bones are pulled out of their sockets and joints.
- "My heart has turned to wax; it has melted away…"
- "My strength is dried up like a potsherd". A potsherd is pottery that is dried and cracked.
- "My tongue sticks to the roof of my mouth". Crucifixion caused severe dehydration. The tongue would stick to the mouth.
- "You lay me in the dust of death. Dogs have surrounded me; a band of evil men has encircled me, they have pierced my hands and my feet".
- It is very interesting to realise that the Hebrew or Jewish people knew nothing of crucifixion a thousand years before Jesus was born. The death penalty in the Law of Moses was stoning. Yet David, the Psalmist, wrote a perfect description of a victim being crucified.
- "I can count all my bones".

- "People stare and gloat over me". This refers to the nakedness of those who were crucified.
- "They divide my garments among them and cast lots for my clothing." This was a reference to the Roman soldiers who perfectly fulfilled this prophecy.

"But You, O LORD, be not far off; O my strength, come quickly to help me. Deliver my life from the sword, my precious life from the power of the dogs. Rescue me from the mouth of the lions; save me from the horns of the wild oxen." Psalm 22:19-21.

This is the alternate thought. Jesus goes from His anguish to remembering what He knows is true about God and He cries out the words of verse 19. At the end of verse 21 is a key statement, when Jesus said:

"Save me." Psalm 22:21

It could also be translated "You have heard me."

Jesus changed from the anguish of feeling that He was forsaken, despised, a worm and that God did not hear Him, to the realisation that God had indeed heard His cry. At this point the Psalm turns and we go from:

- The ANGUISH of the cross

To

- The TRIUMPH of the cross.

Jesus now says that for the rest of eternity the cross will be the TRIUMPH of God. Read His wonderful words:

"I will declare your name to my brothers; in all the congregation I will praise you. You who fear the Lord, praise him! All you descendants of Jacob, honour him! Revere him, all you descendants of Israel! For he has not despised or disdained the suffering of the afflicted one; he has not hidden his face from him but has listened to his cry for help." Psalm 22:22-24.

Imagine Jesus hanging on the cross for many hours. He has gone through the ANGUISH revealed in Psalm 22: 1-21. Maybe, in the last minutes of His life on the cross Jesus begins to rehearse the TRIUMPH of the cross, aware of what He is accomplishing by His death, because in verses 25 and 26 He says:

- "From You comes the theme of my praise in the great assembly."
  The cross will always be the focal point of the worship of God's people.
- "Before those who fear you will I fulfil my vows."
  The cross will become the motivation for our service and our offerings.
- "The poor will eat and be satisfied."
  The cross will provide that which satisfies the restless soul.
- "They who seek the Lord will praise him – may your hearts live forever!"

The Cross will always be:

- The only basis by which we gain eternal life.
- That centrepiece upon which the people of God will:

  - Worship.
  - Serve
  - Bring their offerings.

- The only basis of our eternal life.
- The only basis by which our restless souls find rest.

"All the ends of the earth will remember and turn to the LORD, and all the families of the nations will bow down before him, for dominion belongs to the Lord and he rules over the nations. All the rich of the earth will feast and worship; all who go down to the dust will kneel before him—those who cannot keep themselves alive. Posterity will serve him; future generations will be told about the Lord. They will proclaim his righteousness to a people yet unborn - for he has done it." Psalm 22:27-31.

From verses 27-31 the Psalmist says that on the basis of the cross:

- The people of God from every tribe and tongue and nation will come to the cross. They will come together and worship Him.
- The rich of the earth will feast and worship. All who go down to the dust will kneel before Him. Those who cannot keep themselves alive.
- The rich, the poor, the diseased and the dying will all come to the cross as the basis of their salvation.
- Posterity will serve Him.
- Future generations will be told about the Lord. They will proclaim His righteousness to a people yet unborn. They will proclaim:

"that He has done it." Psalm 22:31.

Generation after generation after generation will come back to the cross, to that moment when Jesus died, as the basis of their salvation and the focal point of their worship.

The last line of verse 31, *"that He has done it,"* could be translated: "It is finished."

You are aware that when Jesus hung on the cross, the last words He uttered were, "It is finished". It was as if He had processed through Psalm 22, rehearsed the TRIUMPH of the cross and concluded that the work was completed. It is actually an accounting term that means: "Paid in full."

Jesus went through the ANGUISH of the cross and the separation from the Father, becoming a worm, despised and rejected. But He remembered the faithfulness of God and that God had brought Him to this point to accomplish His purpose. Then He moved to the TRIUMPH of the cross.

The cross would be remembered for the rest of eternity as the basis by which the people of God worship and serve, bring their offerings and have eternal life. It would be the only basis by which the nations of the world would come together as one people. It would be the focal point of history and with that having been accomplished, Jesus said, "It is finished." And He died.

What about the millions of people who live lives of desperate hopelessness and who flock to temples hoping someday to gain the favour of their manmade gods?

They need to be told that "It is finished."

What about the millions of people who are caught up in religious rituals hoping somehow to please God and merit salvation?

They need to be told that "It is finished."

Those who struggle with restless souls need to know that "It is finished". The work of salvation has been accomplished. God Himself made the sacrifice that we might have life. That is the message of the cross. There is nothing more we need to do.

There is nothing we need to prove. It is finished!

The hymn writer Isaac Watts, conscious of his sin and worthlessness in the sight of a Holy God, asked three questions about His Saviour's willingness to shed His precious blood and to die so that he could be saved. He wrote:

Alas! and did my Saviour bleed?
And did my sovereign die?
Would He devote that sacred Head
for such a worm as I?

The answer is yes, He did!

And it is forever finished.

Chapter 15   Malachi 1:1-14

How Have You Loved Us?

Charles Shultz, creator and author of the Peanuts comic strip, often conveys a Christian message in his humour. In one strip, he conveyed through Charlie Brown the need we all have to be loved. Charlie Brown and Lucy are leaning over the fence speaking to one another:

Charlie Brown: *"All it would take to make me happy is to have someone say he likes me."*
Lucy: *"Are you sure?"*
Charlie Brown: *"Of course I am sure!"*
Lucy: *"You mean you would be happy if someone merely said he or she likes you? Do you mean to tell me that someone has it within his or her power to make you happy merely by doing such a simple thing?"*
Charlie Brown: *"Yes! That is exactly what I mean."*
Lucy: *"Well, I do not think that is asking too much. I really do not."*
Standing face to face, Lucy asks one more time, *"But you are sure now? All you want is to have someone say, 'I like you, Charlie Brown,' and then you will be happy?"*
Charlie Brown: *"And then I will be happy!"*
Lucy turns and walks away saying, *"I cannot do it!"*

The need expressed by Charlie Brown is one that we all feel. We need to be:

- Liked
- Loved
- Accepted

As a result, we do lots of things to try to get these three

things from people around us but we sometimes find ourselves rejected. Fortunately, there is Someone who is always willing to say to us: "I love you! Not because of what you have done. Not because of what you are going to do. Because you are My child, I love you unconditionally. And nothing can ever happen that will ever change that. Even if you mess up, I will still love you. Even if you do not love Me in return, I will still love you."

Charles Schultz was right when he put those words in Charlie Brown's mouth. That is all we need to know in order to be happy. What Lucy was unable, or unwilling, to do for Charlie Brown, God has done for us and it makes a difference in how we:

- See ourselves.
- Relate to God.
- Relate to the people around us.

This is the point that God wanted to make to His people in the days of the Malachi. Let us look at the Scriptures:

An oracle: The word of the LORD to Israel through Malachi. "I have loved you," says the LORD. "But you ask, 'How have you loved us?' "Was not Esau Jacob's brother?" the LORD says. "Yet I have loved Jacob, but Esau I have hated, and I have turned his mountains into a wasteland and left his inheritance to the desert jackals." Edom may say, "Though we have been crushed, we will rebuild the ruins." But this is what the LORD Almighty says: "They may build, but I will demolish. They will be called the Wicked Land, a people always under the wrath of the LORD. You will see it with your own eyes and say, 'Great is the LORD—even beyond the borders of Israel!' "A son honors his father, and a servant his master. If I am a father, where is the honor due me? If I am a master, where is the respect due me?" says the LORD Almighty. "It is you, O priests, who show contempt for my name. "But you ask, 'How have we shown contempt for your name?' "You place defiled food on my altar. But you ask, 'How have we defiled you?' "By saying that the LORD'S table is contemptible. When you bring blind animals for sacrifice, is that not wrong? When you sacrifice crippled or diseased animals, is that not wrong? Try offering them to your governor! Would he be pleased with you? Would he accept you?" says the LORD Almighty. "Now implore God to be gracious to us. With such offerings from your hands, will he accept you?" says the LORD Almighty. "Oh, that one of you would shut the temple doors, so that you would not light useless fires on my altar! I am not pleased with you," says the LORD Almighty, "and I will accept no offering from your hands. My name will be great among the nations, from the rising to the setting of the sun. In every place incense and pure offerings will be brought to my name, because my name will be great among the nations," says the LORD Almighty. "But you profane it by saying of the Lord's table, 'It is defiled,' and of its food, 'It is contemptible.' And you say, 'What a burden!' and you sniff at it contemptuously," says the LORD Almighty. "When you bring injured, crippled or diseased animals and offer them as sacrifices, should I accept them from your hands?" says the LORD. "Cursed is the cheat who has an acceptable male in his flock and vows to give it, but then sacrifices a blemished animal to the Lord. For I am a great king," says the LORD Almighty, "and my name is to be feared among the nations." Mal 1:1-14.

The opening verse is packed full of information that will help to give us a framework for our study together: "An oracle: The word of the LORD to Israel through Malachi." An oracle is actually a "burden." The words to follow in Malachi are not light or trifling but weighty and substantial. Jeremiah wrote:

"Is not my word like fire, declares the LORD, and like a hammer that breaks a rock in pieces?" Jeremiah 23:29.

These words are not just the musings of Malachi but are instead a revelation. God had something He wanted to communicate to His people 2,400 years ago and He wants to use these same words to speak to us today. While the Word of the Lord is heavy, notice that it is written not "against" Israel but "to" them. God was not out to blast them. He wanted to bring them back.

Let us get the history. In 586 B.C., Nebuchadnezzar and the Babylonian army, which we know today as the Iraqi army, defeated the Jews. Jerusalem was destroyed, the walls were demolished and the Temple was burned. The Jewish people were deported and forced into slavery. Many of God's prophets had predicted that this captivity would not destroy the Jewish Nation. It would eventually end and the people would be allowed to return home. They returned at various times although many decided to stay. The last three books of the Old Testament, Haggai, Zechariah and Malachi, were all written after the return from captivity. This was a fulfilment of the prophecy in Jeremiah:

"But when the seventy years are fulfilled, I will punish the king of Babylon and his nation, the land of the Babylonians, for their guilt," declares the Lord, "and will make it desolate forever." Jeremiah 25:12.

The last return came under the leadership of Nehemiah, who led the people to rebuild the walls around Jerusalem. At this time God chose to bring His message through a man named Malachi, whose name means "my messenger." We do not know much more about him except to say that God raised him up with a specific task in mind. Those of God's people who returned were disappointed and discouraged. They had returned to the Promised Land and had rebuilt Jerusalem, replanted their fields, and reconstructed the Temple but life was not going very well.

Their zeal had fizzled out, their faith had turned to an empty formalism and their spirituality was sloppy. They were lethargic, lax and lenient, excusing their own and their leaders' exploits while accusing God of some pretty horrible things. Malachi teaches us what can happen when we are sliding spiritually. The people blamed God for everything and themselves for nothing. Malachi's mandate was to call the people back to a vibrant relationship with the living Lord.

The format of Malachi 1 is the "didactic-dialectic" style:

God's Declaration: *"I have loved you..."*
The peoples' Question: *"How have you loved us?"*
God's Response: *"Was not Esau Jacob's brother...yet I have loved Jacob..."*

I love how verse 2 begins. Instead of lambasting His people, God declares His love for them. "I have loved you,' says the Lord." He does not say. "You are guilty of this or that." God begins with their relationship to Him. The word "love" is in the perfect tense, indicating that God not only loved them in the past but loves them in the present as well. We could say it this way: "I have loved and do love you." And the word God chooses for "love" is not the normal Old Testament term that describes "tough love" or "covenant love." The word God uses here is more relational: "I have embraced you. I have expressed my affection for you," says the Lord. In the book, "The Sacred Romance," authors Brent Curtis and John Eldredge write:

"God is courting us, as He pursues us with His love and calls us to a journey full of intimacy, adventure and beauty. To ignore this whispered call is to become one of the living dead who carry on their lives divorced from their heart."

Sometimes we wrongly or artificially separate the Bible into two by stating that the Old Testament is about law and the New Testament is about love. We need to remember that God's love is part of His character and therefore it permeates both parts of the Bible. So you will read in the Old Testament verses such as:

- "Since you are precious and honoured in my sight, and because I love you…" Isaiah 43:4.
- "I have loved you with an everlasting love; I have drawn you with loving-kindness." Jeremiah 31:3.
- "The LORD your God is with you, he is mighty to save. He will take great delight in you, he will quiet you with his love, he will rejoice over you with singing." Zephaniah 3:17.

What does it mean when we read that God loves us? There are three important aspects of God's love that we should always remember. God's love is:

- Sovereign. God chooses to love us.
- Unconditional. We have done nothing to deserve it
- Committed to us. God loves us even when we mess up.

What a contrast there is between divine and human love.

I love Philip Yancey's perspective in his book, *"What's So Amazing About Grace,"* when he states that:

"There is nothing we can do to make God love us more and there is nothing we can do to make Him love us less. Also, never forget that His love is personal. He knows your name."

Max Lucado puts it this way:

"If God had a refrigerator, your picture would be on it…you are valuable because you exist. Not because of what you do or what you have done, but simply because you are."

In the light of God's love for His people, it seems audacious for them to question His commitment to them, yet, that is what they do in the second part of verse 2. They ask: *"How have you loved us?"* It seems that people wondered why they had to struggle so much when:

- Ezekiel said that the land would abound with fruitfulness but they had to deal with droughts.
- Isaiah prophesied that the population would swell to a mighty throng and that all nations would come and serve them. Yet they were still pretty small and were under a foreign power.

What they did not realise and what the prophet Haggai pointed out to them, was that it was their disobedience that was keeping them from these promised blessings. The people may have thought they were just complaining to Malachi but they were demonstrating their utter disbelief in God and they thought that they could get away with it.

Did the people really think that they could get away with disputing God's love? Before we get too tough on them, let us remember that we do the same thing. When things get tough for us, when someone hurts us, when we are sick, when someone close to us dies or when things do not go as planned, it is very easy to question God's love. When we are wiped out we wonder if God even cares.

Basically, the people were saying: "God, we do not think you love us because if you did we would not be struggling so much." Do you ever think something like that? It is almost as if they were asking: "God, what have you done for us lately"? The people had become so indifferent and so unresponsive to God that they even questioned His love, one of God's core attributes.

Is God's love for us a burden to Him because of our rebellious nature, our hardness of heart and our ingratitude? God had every right at this point to call His people stupid and pronounce judgment on their lack of faith. But He does not. Instead, He gives them a history lesson to demonstrate His love for them.

Look at the last part of verse 2 through to verse 4 for God's answer:

"Was not Esau Jacob's brother?" The Lord says, "Yet I have loved Jacob but Esau I have hated, and I have turned his mountains into a wasteland and left his inheritance to the desert jackals." Edom may say, 'Though we have been crushed, we will rebuild the ruins.' But this is what the LORD Almighty says: 'They may build, but I will demolish. They will be called the Wicked Land, a people always under the wrath of the LORD.'" Malachi 1:2-4.

We cannot go into a detailed description of the relationship between Esau and Jacob now but I do want to hit a few highlights:

- These twin brothers were the sons of Isaac.
- Esau, the eldest, should have been the main heir of Isaac's blessings.
- God chose the younger son Jacob to be the main heir.
- The Jewish people were descended from Jacob.
- Because God chose Jacob, the people in Malachi's day were God's chosen people as well.

Many stumble over verse 3: "But Esau I have hated..."

Here are a few things to remember that may help us

understand the meaning of this strong statement.

- In his heart, Jacob hungered after God. Even though he was a schemer and a scoundrel, as he matured in his faith, he grew to trust God. Esau, on the other hand, placed no value on spiritual matters at all.
- The words "love" and "hate" should be used in a relative sense. In the Hebrew idiom, if a father had two sons and gave one the inheritance, it was said that he loved one and hated the other.

The question for us as we study Malachi is not why God rejected Esau but why he chose Jacob:

- God elected to lavish mercy on the deceiver Jacob, even though he deserved justice.
- Esau simply received what was coming to him.
- Without mercy, Jacob would have been passed over as well.
- Esau's descendents became the Edomites, because they lived in a land called Edom.

In verse 3, God declares about the Edomites that He has, "turned his mountains into a wasteland and left his inheritance to the desert jackals." There are several reasons why God judged the Edomites:

- They refused to allow Moses passage after the Israelites left Egypt.
- Many of Israel's Kings fought against the Edomites over the years.
- Edom did not offer to help Judah when the Babylonians invaded them and they looted Jerusalem after her destruction.

God now ends the history lesson He was giving to His people to demonstrate His love for them. The people had questioned God's love because He had allowed the Babylonians to take them captive and permitted the Edomites to ignore their distress and add to their sorrow. Here is God's answer to their complaint: "I have proved my love for you by choosing Jacob over Esau. I returned you to your land and destroyed the Edomites. What more evidence of my love do you need"? God declares His love for us too and then demonstrates it when we dispute His devotion. He goes out of His way to let us know how much He loves us and yet He does not want us to keep that love to ourselves. Look at verse 5:

"You will see it with your own eyes and say, 'Great is the LORD, even beyond the borders of Israel!'" Malachi 1.5.

The Israelites were indifferent and insensitive to God's love but a day is coming when they will be forced to acknowledge it. Did you know that there is something about love that urges us to respond? Maybe you have been blaming God for some pretty tough thing that has happened to you. Perhaps you are you not sure if God really loves you. Will you respond to Him today?

Because the people did not respond to God's love, things started to go wrong for them. We see that:

- Their worship was unspiritual routine.
- Their leaders were unspiritual men.
- Their family relationships ruptured with divorce high on their agendas.
- Their offerings were worthless animals that had deformities.
- In reality, they had stopped serving God.

To help us understand how bad their attitude was to a God who had always loved and cared for them and who would always do so, think of the beginning and the end of Malachi as two bookends. At one end is the beautiful statement found in verse 2 of Chapter 1:

> "I have loved you." Malachi 1:2.

At the other end we find wonderful promises in verse 2 of Chapter 4:

> "But for you who revere my name, the sun of righteousness will rise with healing in its wings. And you will go out and leap like calves released from the stall." Malachi 4:2.

The prophecy of Malachi begins with God's love for them in the present and ends with God's wonderful promises for their future. And everything in between is God's programme to get them to achieve His objective for them. As part of His programme for our spiritual progress, God longs for us to give Him our best so that we can experience His love in a richer fuller way. Let us focus on three ways we can do that.

We need to embrace an authentic faith, give God priority over our possessions and grasp the greatness of God.

FIRST: We must embrace an authentic faith

> "A son honours his father, and a servant his master. If I am a father, where is the honour due me? If I am a master, where is the respect due me? says the LORD Almighty." Malachi 1:6.

What we see right away in verse 6 is that God describes Himself both as a Father and a Master and there are two sides to His love.

- One side is tender.
- The other side is tougher.

The Father is:

- Relational in His giving.
- Resplendent in His glory.

As such we must honour Him. Because we are the Father's children and servants of the Master, we should have:

- Security in the Father's care for us.
- Reverence for His authority. Seven times in Chapter 1 verses 6 to 14 and twenty-three times in Malachi, God calls Himself: "The Lord Almighty."

Look at the first half of verse 6. You can almost hear the priests saying: *"Amen, that is right God. Bring it on. Let the people have it."* But notice the second half of the verse. God said: "It is you, O priests, who show contempt for my name." Ouch. Now it is time for the priests to listen.

By the way, this had to be a difficult message for Malachi to deliver because he was not a priest. The priests probably resented him and looked down upon him. They certainly did not like what he had to say.

The priests showed *"contempt"* for God, which means that they no longer thought of Him as weighty. They despised their duties and scorned the sacred because worship had become wearisome and they took God for granted. And, they had the nerve to lash out at the Lord of Hosts. Look at the priests' question in the last part of verse 6: "How have we shown contempt for your name?" Whenever you ask

God "how," He will tell you. In verse 7, He answered them: "You place defiled food on my altar." Unbelievably, the priests persisted in their questioning: "How have we defiled you?" God replied: "By saying that the Lord's Table is contemptible."

The priests were just going through the motions like we sometimes do when we allow the extraordinary to become ordinary. In fact, intimate familiarity with the holy can lead to low level spirituality if we are not careful. If God bores you, then nothing else is going to satisfy you. If we want to give God our best we must:

- Embrace God's authenticity.
- Be genuine and stop going through the motions of worship and service.
- Stop playing church.
- Do whatever it takes to keep the fire burning.

Some of us dishonour God and count Him contemptible when we try to live on what Charles Swindoll calls, "three dollars' worth of God." He writes:

"Some of us would love to buy three dollars worth of God. Not enough to explode my soul or disturb my sleep, but just enough to equal a cup of warm milk or a snooze in the sunshine...I want ecstasy, not transformation. I want the warmth of the womb, not new birth. I want a pound of the eternal in a paper sack. I want three dollars worth of God, please."

To make progress in experiencing God's love, embrace an authentic faith.

SECOND: God's priority over our possessions

"'When you bring blind animals for sacrifice, is that not wrong? When you sacrifice crippled or diseased animals, is that not wrong? Try offering them to your governor! Would he be pleased with you? Would he accept you?' says the LORD Almighty." Malachi 1:8.

What did the people bring to God? Was it their second best? No, it was much worse than that. They brought sick sheep and gross goats and the priests were accepting these animals. They were offering animals that were valueless. Imagine the parade of diseased animals limping and stumbling blindly toward the Temple, their oozing sores covered with flies. The reason God says, *"is that not wrong?"* twice in this verse is because the people and certainly the priests, must have known better.

Here is the principle. God deserves priority over your possessions.

The people were more concerned with keeping what they had than they were with giving God their best. Their hearts were not in it. They were still coming to church but it was just a meaningless ritual to them. They had accepted mediocrity in their lives and their leaders did nothing about it. God told them to try and offer their junk to the governor as payment of their taxes and see if he would be pleased with them and accept them.

The bottom line is they thought that God did not care what they did. They probably thought:

- We have worked hard for what we have.
- We have to pay high taxes.
- We have a lot of bills to pay.
- We have no cash to spare.

I am challenged by this passage because the priests might

have tried to excuse themselves by saying:

- ❏ It is not our fault.
- ❏ We are just sacrificing what the people give to us.
- ❏ We have no animals of our own to sacrifice.
- ❏ There are no perfect animals for us to sacrifice because the people only bring their leftovers to God.

God did not accept any excuses from the priests. He held the priests accountable for what the people brought. That was God's response then. What would God's response be today? He holds those who lead churches accountable to ensure that the church does not slip into a ritualistic religion where Christians no longer give God their best.

One of the best ways to monitor how you are doing spiritually is to take a look at your giving: Are you:

- ❏ Leaving God your leftovers?
- ❏ Giving God priority over your possessions?

Let us come to the third way in which we can respond to God and experience His love.

THIRD: We must grasp the greatness of God.

Verse 10 should cause us to sit bolt upright in our chairs. God would much rather we shut down our churches than come to Him with pathetic leftovers:

"Oh, that one of you would shut the temple doors, so that you would not light useless fires on my altar! I am not pleased with you, says the LORD Almighty, and I will accept no offering from your hands." Malachi 1:10.

How would you feel if when you go to your church the

doors were locked and the building was sealed? As hard as this may be to hear, God does not need our sacrifices. God does not need us to give Him anything. He is saying to us: *"I had rather you shut everything down than have you represent Me as some lifeless religious icon and continue in a phoney religious ritual. If you are not prepared to give Me every inch of your life, then you cannot play church because I am closing the doors."* This stings but no worship at all is better than half-hearted sacrifice. This passage gives us the purpose behind offerings. Read verses 11 and 14 and see if you can detect it:

"My name will be great among the nations, from the rising to the setting of the sun. In every place incense and pure offerings will be brought to my name, because my name will be great among the nations, says the LORD Almighty." Malachi 1:11.

"Cursed is the cheat who has an acceptable male in his flock and vows to give it, but then sacrifices a blemished animal to the Lord. For I am a great king, says the LORD Almighty, and my name is to be feared among the nations." Malachi 1:14.

Notice how that every time God mentioned sacrifice, He followed it with the phrase: *"I will be great"* or *"I will be feared."* Sacrifice is directly linked to the greatness of God. That is why when we give Him our best we are grasping the greatness of God. Conversely, when we offer Him little or nothing, we are really saying that God does not matter much to us. When we fail to celebrate God's greatness by giving Him our best, our priorities go out of whack and we become bored with God and excited about the world.

Have you ever noticed that there is no one more miserable than a half-hearted Christian? That is what happened to the priests. Instead of counting it a privilege to minister on God's behalf, they exclaimed:

"What a burden!" Malachi 1:13.

In their minds it was more trouble than it was worth. They

"sniffed at it contemptuously." Malachi 1:13.

They even "puffed" or "blew" in exaggerated exasperation. I imagine God looking at us and wondering why we get so bored with Him. God actually put this into a question in the days of Micah, another Old Testament Prophet: "My people, what have I done to you? How have I burdened you? Answer me." Micah 6:3.

And in the time of the Prophet Isaiah we hear an extreme exclamation from the Almighty:

"When you come to appear before me, who has asked this of you, this trampling of my courts? Stop bringing meaningless offerings! Your incense is detestable to me." Isaiah 1:12-13.

Notice the strong words in the first chapter of Malachi:

"Cursed is the cheat who has an acceptable male in his flock and vows to give it, but then sacrifices a blemished animal to the Lord." Malachi 1:14.

God not only wanted the Temple shut down but He warned that any person who offered blemished animals would be bitterly cursed. No wonder the Lord was angry.

The people promised to give Him their best but then they gave Him their worst. God is saying that His Name will be great, whether we acknowledge it or not. God warned Israel that His greatness and His grace would be given to the Gentiles and that is what is happening now. And, there is a time coming when every knee will acknowledge His supremacy.

There are three symptoms of wearisome worship in the Church today. They are:

- Inadequate preparation.
- Half-hearted participation.
- Improper motivation.

Let us look at each one more closely.

One: Inadequate Preparation

This touches on what happens before the service begins. Have you ever wondered why the Jewish Sabbath begins on a Friday evening at sundown? It is because preparation for worship begins the night before.

Are you taking time on Saturday night to get yourself ready for Sunday?

Two: Half-hearted Participation

This relates to what we do when we get to church. Because we generally know what is going to happen in a service it is easy to just go through the motions.

There is nothing more boring than trying to worship God when your heart is not in it.

The people at the front are not there to entertain us. They are there to assist us in our personal worship because we are not the audience. God is.

Three: Improper Motivation

This touches on the reason we attend church in the first place. Do you go to:

- Get something for yourself?
- Keep an appointment with God?
- Give God your personal worship?

Your answers make a world of difference. Instead of wondering if a church service helped you or determining if you *liked* it or not, the real issues are these:

- Did I meet with God?
- Did I grasp to some degree His greatness?

Maybe we need to take time to assess our spiritual behaviour and ask ourselves some practical, perhaps awkward, questions. Are we giving God:

- Our time?
- The best of our talents?
- Our treasures?

Or, like the people in Malachi's day, are we giving God our leftovers? If we are going to give God our best, we must first grasp His greatness and embrace an authentic faith. Instead of questioning God's love, we will experience it.

It all comes down to this. When we get a glimpse of the greatness of God, and what Jesus has done for us, we will never play church again. We will give God our best for the rest of our lives and never need to question God's love for us.

Chapter 16   Revelation 5

Who is worthy to break the seals and open the scroll?

If you have read this book from the beginning, you will have noted that in the previous chapters of this book we have picked out a wide selection of questions that are asked in the Bible. Some questions were asked by God of people, some asked by people of God, some asked by prophets or apostles or people like us. Now, in the last book of the New Testament, we are looking at a great question asked by angels.

> "Who is worthy to break the seals and open the scroll?"
> Revelation 5:2.

The Book of Revelation is the only book in the Bible that promises a special blessing to those who read it, hear it and study it. The book is divided very simply into three separate parts:

- Past.
- Present.
- Future.

Are you ready to meet the Lord? You had better be because there is nothing in God's prophetic calendar that needs to be fulfilled for Jesus Christ to return.

Let me tell you a true amusing story as an introduction.

A pastor was talking about his grandmother. She was one of

those great, godly women who shone with the presence of the Holy Spirit. She lived during the financial difficulties of the 1930s and was always helping to feed needy people. She never turned people away from her door. She always told them about the Lord and then she always fed them lunch if they were hungry. An old man came to her door and asked for some food. She invited him in and he sat down there at the dinner table. She got out some ham and started cutting some pieces for him. Suddenly, she remembered, "I have not talked to him about the Lord yet." She whirled around and confronted him right into his face and said: "Sir, are you ready to meet the Lord?" It scared him so much he knocked his chair over, ran straight through the door and went off running down the railway track. She said to her husband: "What got into him?" He said: "Dear, look, you are holding a butcher knife in your hand."

In Revelation 5 John says:

"...I saw in the right hand of him who sat on the throne a scroll with writing on both sides and sealed with seven seals. And I saw a mighty angel proclaiming in a loud voice, 'Who is worthy to break the seals and open the scroll?'" Revelation 5:1-2

REVEALING THE BOOK

Its characteristics: a scroll with seven seals

When we think of a book, we think of a book bound on one side but books with binding did not exist until about the third century after Jesus. In fact, Christian preachers took Old Testament scrolls and tied them together on the ends. They were the forerunners of our books. They only had scrolls in Bible days.

I remember being in Jerusalem and going to the Museum of the Dead Sea Scrolls. Around the walls of that Museum is a 13 metre long scroll of the Book of Isaiah. Back in

Bible times, they mashed reeds to create papyrus, a form of paper. That is what a scroll was made of. Sometimes they rolled a scroll up and then put it in another scroll. This is what John saw in Heaven. It was a rolled up scroll with seven seals on the top.

We do not know exactly what the seals looked like but when you opened the scroll and broke the first seal, you unwound the first section. The Bible says that there was writing on the outside of the scroll as well as on the inside so, after the first seal was broken, what was written on the scroll could be read.

It could be that one side of the scroll tells us what events are happening in Heaven while the other side of the scroll tells us what events are happening at the same time on Earth. The different seals will be broken at a predetermined time. What is written on the pages will be shared. You can see how it would happen. It was rolled up as one scroll. The first seal was broken and the first page could be read. Then, when the second seal was broken, the second page could be read. That is how the seven seals are contained in that scroll.

John had a vision that he was in Heaven with all the redeemed of all the ages. He heard an angel ask if any of those present were worthy to take the scroll and to open the seven seals

Its contents: a scroll with writing on both sides

Now this is something that will bless your heart but you will have to understand a little Old Testament history. This scroll represents our forfeited inheritance. It is what God originally intended for Adam and Eve and for you and for me. But we forfeited our inheritance because of sin.

There are some vital matters that we must note:

- We personally cannot buy back or redeem the inheritance that we have forfeited because of sin.
- The forfeited inheritance can be bought back or redeemed for us but we need to find someone who can act on our behalf.

The one who acts for us must fulfil three legal requirements. They must:

- Have the legal authority to act on our behalf.
- Be our kinsman, be related to us.
- Be able to pay the full price that is required.

One who fulfils all these legal requirements is called in the Bible a legal kinsman, in Hebrew a *go'el which* means "a redeemer kinsman." Only a legal kinsman can buy back or redeem the inheritance that we forfeited through sin.

Many of you are familiar with the Book of Ruth in the Old Testament. It is the story of Naomi, who went to live in a foreign land. Her husband and two sons died there, leaving Naomi and her two daughters-in-law alone. One of the daughters-in-law went back to her own people but Ruth stayed with Naomi and eventually Naomi moved back to her homeland and Ruth goes with her.

Here is the problem. There was land which was once owned by Naomi's family but Naomi cannot buy it back because only a male could purchase land in those days. So she needed a male redeemer kinsman. Ruth cannot buy it back because she was also a woman. So they need someone who could buy it back for them as a legal kinsman and this was a real problem to them. Let me tell you something about Hebrew law relating to land.

The law in those days decreed that land always belonged to a family, so a family never gave away their legal ownership to it. If a family fell on hard times and they had to give up the land because they were in debt and needed money, someone could pay a sum of money to possess or occupy the land but the legal ownership of the land was always preserved for the family. The family's right of ownership was written in a document that we know today as the Title Deed. At any time in the future, no matter how many generations afterwards, a kinsman, a true relative of the original owner could come to the one who possessed or occupied the property and if he could prove that he was a legal kinsman, he could buy the property back for the sum of money paid for the land to the family and claim the Title Deed.

In other words, if you bought land from somebody who was not in your family, you always stood the risk of a legal kinsman returning and claiming his right to it. The family's rights were always contained in some kind of a sealed document of title like the scroll we have mentioned earlier. But only a legal kinsman who could pay the full purchase price could redeem the land and obtain the Title Deed to it.

In the story of Ruth that is exactly what happened. A fine-looking man named Boaz came on the scene. Ruth started noticing Boaz and Boaz started noticing Ruth. Of course, Naomi did what a lot of women like to do, she played matchmaker. She told Ruth where Boaz would be and told her to get cleaned up, fix her hair, put on fresh makeup and go down there and put some moves on him. That is a loose translation of the original Hebrew. So ladies you ought to read the Book of Ruth. This is how she caught him. She went and slept at his feet all night. Boaz was so honoured by that.

Boaz was not the only legal kinsman neither was he the first one in line. There was another and he also wanted the property. If you read the Book of Ruth you will see that Boaz went up to the man who was number one in line, the closest relative and he said to him: "If you get the property, you get Ruth also. You have to take the woman with the property." I like the tactful way this man answered. He said: "Well, I cannot do that. It would kind of mess up my family." Probably meaning, "I already have a wife and she would not dare let me get another one." So he said: "All right. I give up my claim." Then Boaz said: "I claim my rights as the legal kinsman." Boaz married Ruth and he obtained the Title Deed, the scroll, because he was the *go'el*, the legal redeemer kinsman.

This true Old Testament story with its happy ending takes us back to Revelation Chapter 5 and the question being asked by the angel who wanted to know: "Is there a redeemer kinsman who is worthy to redeem what mankind forfeited when they sinned?" We know the answer to that question. You and I know that Jesus is the only One who can do that. That is why we sing: "Redeemed by the blood of the Lamb. I have been redeemed!" But, do you know the meaning of that word "redeemed"? It means: "I have been bought back!"

You say, "But wait a minute Derek. I am confused about the tenses you have been using to explain the chapter. Can you clarify some of your points for me?

- Are we learning about a future event or one that occurred in the past?
- Surely you are teaching about an event that will take place in the future after Jesus has returned to take us to Heaven?
- You started this chapter by mentioning that Jesus was

coming back and you asked us if we were ready to meet Him but you have referred to our redemption as a past event.
- You are right about what we sing. We always sing about our redemption in the past tense, for example, "I have been redeemed".

Let me explain it like this.

Jesus has already:

- Redeemed us.
- Paid the price on Calvary.

But, Jesus has not yet claimed the Title Deed, the scroll. When the Bible speaks of the Second Coming of Jesus, the Bible uses the future tense. For example:

"When these things begin to take place, stand up and lift your heads, because your redemption is drawing near." Luke 21:28.

In a real sense our redemption has not been *completed* until Jesus takes the Title Deed scroll.

In summary, the book is a scroll with seven seals and it is the Title Deed to what God intended for mankind, our redemption.

THE REACTION TO THE BOOK

"But no one in heaven or on earth or under the earth could open the scroll or even look inside it." John says, "I wept and wept because no one was found who was worthy to open the scroll or look inside. Then one of the elders said to me, 'Do not weep! See, the Lion of the tribe of Judah, the Root of David, has triumphed. He is able to open the scroll and its seven seals." Revelation 5:3-5.

The First Reaction: a futile search

The search was thorough. Look at the extent of it:

- In Heaven.
- On Earth.
- Under the Earth.

Consider the comprehensive nature of this search. Look at the potential candidates. Is there "anyone"? When you think of the places that were searched and the fact that everyone in those places was considered, that was some extensive search. Extensive or not, it was unsuccessful because no one was found:

- Who was worthy
- Who could pay the price
- Who could prove His relationship to the original owner
- Who could open the scroll or look inside it

John realised that the search had been futile and he concluded:

- Nobody in Heaven could do it.
- Nobody on Earth who was left behind when Jesus returned could do it.
- Nobody in Hell could do it.
- Nobody.

The Second Reaction: a fearful sadness

Did you expect to see tears in Heaven? Has anybody ever

told you there will not be any tears in Heaven? That is not what the Bible says.

The Bible says:

> "And God will wipe away every tear from their eyes." Revelation 7:17.

Then, later on in the New Jerusalem, we read that:

> "...there will be no more death or mourning or crying or pain, for the old order of things has passed away." Revelation 21:4.

But here we read that John was weeping in Heaven. The word for "weeping" is a strong word. It means that John's body was wracked with sobs. Why? Because John thought: *"Well, here it is. Here is mankind's redemption and there is nobody able to come and take it and redeem it."* And so he cried. His tears represent all the tears of sinful man throughout history. Tears never started until sin entered the world. They represent:

- The tears of Adam and Eve as they stood over the grave of their son, Abel.
- The tears of Adam and Eve as they were driven out of Paradise.
- The tears of the Israelites in Egypt making bricks from straw.
- The tears of people through the ages as their loved ones suffer and die.
- They represent all the tears of everyone.

As John's tears were flowing the angel said:

"Do not cry anymore. THERE IS SOMEONE WHO IS WORTHY."

THE RECIPIENT OF THE BOOK

John wrote: "Then I saw a Lamb."

Notice what John heard back in verse 5. The elder said: "See the Lion of the Tribe of Judah, the root of David..."

John saw the Lion that became a Lamb. He noted two matters about the Lion that have great significance. The Lion was "of the Tribe of Judah" and The Root of David." What does this picture tell us?

- We know that the lion is the king of all the beasts.
- The Tribe of Judah was one of the twelve tribes of Israel. This One was born into a Jewish family.
- The "Root of David" means that this One comes from the family of King David, the Jewish Royal Family.
- This One is "The King of Kings".

"He has triumphed."

Notice what John mentions in these verses:

"I saw a Lamb, looking as if it had been slain, standing in the centre of the throne, encircled by the four living creatures and the elders. He had seven horns and seven eyes, which are the seven spirits of God sent out into all the earth. He came and took the scroll from the right hand of him who sat on the throne." (God the Father) "And when he had taken it, the four living creatures and the twenty-four elders fell down before the Lamb. Each one had a harp and they were holding golden bowls full of incense, which are the prayers of the saints."

Notice 1: The Lamb revealed

It is interesting that the Bible says the One on the Throne

is God the Father, God Almighty. It seems as if in Revelation Chapters 4 and 5 the Lord Jesus Christ as the Lamb of God is standing in the edges of the stage. It is not until this point, when He dramatically walks forward and takes the scroll, that the Lamb is revealed. How do we know this Lamb is the Lord Jesus?

- ❏ Because the Bible calls Him the Lamb of God.
- ❏ Jesus was slain for our sins.
- ❏ He is the One who was dead but is now alive.

Let me give you three words that describe Jesus in this picture in Revelation:

- ❏ Slain.
- ❏ Standing.
- ❏ Strong.

FIRST: The word *"slain"*. The Lamb was "looking as if It had been slain." "Slain" was a ceremonial word and described what happened to the lamb on the day of Yom Kippur, the Day of Atonement. The High Priest took a curved, sharp, razor-like blade and slit the throat of the lamb and blood poured out on the altar. There were thousands and thousands of lambs, rams and animals killed before Jesus died on the cross and the Bible says in Hebrews that these sacrifices never cleansed one sin:

"Day after day every priest stands and performs his religious duties; again and again he offers the same sacrifices, which can never take away sins." Hebrews 10:11.

But the death of Jesus cleanses us from all our sins.

SECOND: The word *"standing"*. The Lamb was "standing in the centre." Not only was the Lamb *"slain"* but the

Lamb was *"standing"*. Now you would expect that a dead animal was lying down but the word "standing" tells us that the Lamb is alive.

THIRD: The word *"strong"*. The Lamb is *"strong"*. The Lamb is revealed not only as a Lamb that despite being *"slain"* is *"standing"*, the Lamb is also *strong*. How do we know the Lamb is strong? Look at verse 6:

"He had seven horns and seven eyes which are the seven spirits of God sent out into all the earth."

Now, do not be afraid of the beautiful symbolism in the Book of Revelation. This is symbolic language. You recall from The Gospels that Jesus often used this type of language to illustrate His message. Jesus said "I am the door..." and "I am the vine..." What is significant in verse 6 is the number seven. The Jews applied specific meanings to numbers and so their use of specific numbers to convey information was important. Today your will hear the numbers 24/7 being used to mean every day and 20/20 being used to mean perfect vision. The number seven would signify perfection to the Jews and John referred to seven horns and seven eyes which are the seven spirits of God. The horn was a sign of strength. So when it says that He had seven horns it means that the Lord Jesus was perfect in strength and power. He has all the strength we need. He is able to deliver on every promise. When it says that He has seven eyes which are the seven spirits of God, it is a picture, a symbol of the Holy Spirit. The seven spirits represent the perfect Holy Spirit of God.

In Revelation 5 we see this picture of the Lamb standing there taking the scroll. It is a picture of the Lord Jesus saying: "I am the one! I am the Redeemer Kinsman." The Lord Jesus is the *only* one, the *go'el,* who can take the scroll, which is the redemption we forfeited through sin and buy it back for us because:

- He is the Son of the living God.
- He died for us on Calvary.
- He has paid the price of our redemption in full.

Notice 3: The Lamb is revered

I want you to see who else is in Heaven with us:

"And when he had taken it, the four living creatures and the twenty-four elders fell down before the Lamb. Each one had a harp and they were holding golden bowls full of incense, which are the prayers of the saints." Revelation 5:8.

I believe the twenty-four elders represent all the redeemed of all the ages. Every time you see the words "twenty-four elders", substitute the pronoun "us." At that moment, the Bible says that we are going to fall down before the Lamb and worship Him. What is it going to be like in Heaven?

"Each one had a harp."

The Bible says we are all going to have harps and be:

"holding golden bowls full of incense, which are the prayers of the saints."

This is probably symbolic of how all the prayers you have ever prayed are being stored up in Heaven. These prayers are like incense, a sweet smelling aroma that rises up to Heaven.

Did you know that there are a lot of our prayers that have not been fulfilled? In fact, one prayer has not yet been fulfilled:

> "Your will be done on earth as it is in heaven." Matthew 6:10.

Is God's will being done in Heaven? Of course! Is God's will being done on Earth now? No, but it will be then. So, all the prayers you have ever prayed will be there with the twenty-four elders. We then read in verse 9:

> "And *they* sang a new song." Revelation 5:9.

I want to be very careful about this, because I have always taught that angels do not sing. That is, there are no biblical references to angels singing. I want you to notice *who* is singing; it is us, the twenty-four elders.

Let us put ourselves in the future and imagine that we are standing in the very throne-room of God. Jesus has taken the scroll, which pictures our redemption and we have fallen down at His feet. Now let us worship Him:

> "You are worthy to take the scroll and to open its seals. Because you were slain, and with your blood you purchased men for God from every tribe and language and people and nation. You have made them to be a kingdom and priests to serve our God. And they will reign on the earth."
> Revelation 5:9-10.

This is a song we are going to sing. We are going to fall before the Lamb and this is what we are going to sing to Him:

"You are the only One who is worthy because with Your blood, you bought us back. You have redeemed us."

Note what God makes us into:

"...a kingdom and priests to serve our God." Revelation 5:10.

We read in the Old Testament that it was God's intention for the nation of Israel that the priests would be the kings and the kings would be the priests. God never wanted the functions of priest and king to be separated. Those of you who know Old Testament history know that God did permit a king to rule His people as an accommodation to them. They wanted a king because the gentile nations had kings. God always wanted godly kings to rule His people. What does it mean when it says:

"They will reign on the earth?" Revelation 5:10.

This refers to the "millennial reign of Christ on the Earth." We, the redeemed, are going to rule the Earth during those one thousand years.

We are not the only group who are going to worship the Lamb: There is another group:

"And I looked and I heard the voice of many angels, numbering thousands upon thousands and ten thousand times ten thousand." Revelation 5:11.

Imagine that number of angels. It is a number, which literally translates in Greek is *innumerable.* It is the Greek word from which we get our word *myriads.* It is a number so great that it cannot be numbered.

What is the largest number you can think of? A number of years ago there was a physicist who was looking out on his lawn one morning contemplating the innumerable dewdrops on it. He said to his son, "How many dewdrops do you think there are out there?" His son looked out there and he said, "Why, Dad. There must be googles." That is where that number originated. It is an actual number that this nuclear physicist coined. Google means one with a hundred zeroes. Can you imagine google to the hundredth power? It is a number so large, you cannot comprehend it.

The truth of the matter is that the Bible never gives an exact number of angels but it seems that at this time in the future, the angels are no longer required on the Earth ministering to the redeemed because there are none on the Earth. We have all been caught up to Heaven. Not only are we there worshipping the Lamb, the angels are too and:

"They encircled the throne and the living creatures and the elders." Revelation 5:11.

Here is the picture:

- The Throne in the centre with God Almighty on it.
- There is the Lamb of God.

Then, encircling the Throne are:

- The four living creatures.
- The redeemed.
- Innumerable Angels.

The angels began to praise: "in a loud voice they shout."

I want you to be aware that although The NIV and The Living Bible use the word "sang" in verse 12, in the Greek it is the word *lego* which means *"they spoke"* or *"they shouted."*

The word *"lego"* is a totally different word than the word used in verse 9 which has been correctly translated as "sing." So:

- We, the redeemed, will have a new song.
- We will sing our praise. That is verse 9.
- The angels have not sinned and therefore, unlike us, do not need to be redeemed.
- The angels do not sing our new song that speaks about our redemption.
- The angels will shout their praise. That is verse 12.
- This will be the angels' theme as they begin their praise:

"Worthy is the Lamb, who was slain, to receive power and wealth and wisdom and strength and honour and glory and praise!" Revelation 5:12.

Let us continue with the picture:

- Encircling the throne are:

  The four living creatures.
  The redeemed.
  The angels.

- We begin to sing our new song to the Lamb:

  "You are worthy to take the scroll and to open its seals. Because you were slain, and with your blood you purchased men for God from every tribe and language and people and nation. You have made them to be a kingdom and priests to serve our God. And they will reign on the earth." Revelation 5:9,10.

- Then, innumerable hosts of angels encircling us respond with:

"Worthy is the Lamb, who was slain, to receive power and wealth and wisdom and strength and honour and glory and praise." Revelation 5:12.

- There is one further pinnacle of praise:

"Then I heard every creature in heaven and on earth and under the earth and on the sea, and all that is in them, singing: "To him who sits on the throne and to the Lamb be praise and honor and glory and power, forever and ever!" Revelation 5:13.

Verse 13 confirms some very important truths that we must not overlook while we are thinking about and enjoying the wonderful future that Jesus, the Lamb of God, died on the cross at Calvary to secure for us:

- Not everyone will be in Heaven.
- John refers to four places, Heaven, Earth, under the Earth and on the sea.
- Only the redeemed and the angels will be in Heaven giving their praise and honour to God and to the Lamb of God.
- Everyone else, wherever they might be on that day, will add their praise to the praise of the redeemed and the praise of the angels as all give praise and honour to God and to the Lamb of God.
- As we and the angels do now, we will on that day willingly give our praise and honour to our God and the Lamb of God.
- Those who have not been redeemed, those who refuse to acknowledge the worthiness of our God and the Lamb of God now, will have no choice then. It will be too late then for them to join the redeemed in Heaven.

Be certain of this, whatever the unbelievers proudly and

arrogantly say now, they will honour God and the Lamb of God along with the rest of creation then.

I know that today Christians are continually confronted by blasphemy and that the situation is getting worse as youngsters copy adults. I know how much it not only offends but hurts believers. Each time you get upset, offer your praise and worship to your Heavenly Father and pray for the salvation of the blasphemers. I promise that instead of hurting, you will have a time of blessing.

If you think you are going to go to Heaven sit in some corner and be nice and quiet and inactive, get ready because it is going to be a great festival of praise! It is going to be like a Niagara Falls of praise and worship to the Lamb. Start praising the Lord here or you are going to be absolutely out of place there.

Finally, to conclude the picture, we come to verse 14. We have thought about a threefold pinnacle of praise involving:

- First, the four creatures and the redeemed.
- Then the angels.
- Finally everyone.

Then,

"The four living creatures said, "Amen," and the elders fell down and worshipped." Revelation 5:14.

That is beautiful and it is the opposite of what we do now. If a respected person walked in we would stand up but if Jesus Christ walked in we would fall down. Get ready, because when we get to Heaven, we are going to be falling at the feet of the Lamb because He is the only one who is worthy to take back what was once ours. You might have sung for many years: "Worthy is the Lamb that was slain." You now know what He is worthy to do. He is worthy as the Son of God because He paid with His own blood the price required to buy back those who were lost.

You say, Derek: "Who is going to be in Heaven doing all this praising?" I tell you: "All those who are saved when Jesus returns for His Church." You say: "What if I am not a Christian when Jesus returns? Where will I be?" Check Revelation Chapter 6 for the very solemn answer.

If you are a believer, can I ask you to get into the good habit of worshipping and praising Christ now? He is worthy to receive our praise and worship now. In the busy world in which we live, when time for everyone is at a premium, it is essential that we remind ourselves of the importance of worship. Let me ask you a question that will assist you to understand why this is so.

What is the ultimate end for the Church?

- It is not evangelism.
- It is not missions.
- It is WORSHIP.

Let me make this teaching crystal clear:

- The reason we seek the lost is so that they might become worshippers.
- When we worship, we fulfil the very purpose for which we were created.

Worship is a way of life. It is not something we should turn on and off depending on our mood or our circumstances. I do not know your problems and I want to be as helpful as I can. So, let me clarify. Are you or someone special to you:

- Struggling with the loss of a loved one?
- Battling a disease or a terminal illness?
- Struggling with a marriage that is falling apart or children who have gone down a rebellious path?
- Struggling with your job?
- Struggling with despair and hopelessness and depression?

These and problems like them make it so essential to worship. It is because life is lived in the trenches that we need to come back and see God for who He is. We worship because Christ is worthy of our worship but in the process we are reminded of who He is and who we are and how much we need Him. We are reminded of what is eternal and what is temporal. It is so important to get into the practice of offering our personal praise and worship during each day of the week, not just on Sunday. This spiritual time will thrill your heart as you forget yourself and enjoy Christ's presence with you.

We all have views about what should happen when we meet with other Christians to worship together. We all know what we consider appropriate and that is so often determined by our traditions, our personality and by our experiences. So often worship is determined by a lot of things but some may not be biblical. Understand, worship needs to be real, which means it needs to be real to *you*.

When I go to a football game, I do not jump and cheer and yell all the time. I just do not; I am not made that way. For me to go into a church building and jump and cheer and yell all the time would really just be a show. That is not me. I need to worship in a way that is real to me. You need to worship in a way that is real to you. We need to allow one another the freedom to celebrate God in ways that may be different from our way. Let me illustrate this by reference to the music used to assist worship.

Let me tell you about the musical instruments that are used in worship. Experience has taught that these, the choice of hymns and spiritual songs, and the volume of the music, are a constant source of complaint. For some, these problems impede or totally inhibit their time of worship.

I do find it interesting that the psalmist is so clear about this. The last Psalm, Psalm 150, is about Praising the Lord:

"Praise him with the sounding of the trumpet, praise him with the harp and lyre, praise him with tambourine and dancing, praise him with the strings and flute, praise him with the clash of cymbals, praise him with resounding cymbals." Psalm 150:3-5.

Despite these words, the church has for 2000 years been undecided whether or not musical instruments are even appropriate in worship so I want to give you an historical overview:

- Instrumental music in the church began in the Middle Ages, AD 500 to 1450, particularly with the organ. But it was opposed and organs were then removed.
- The churches that did use the organ often met with resistance from the religious leaders.
- It appears that in the Middle Ages the organ and stringed instruments were used but often the church leaders discarded their use and disdained all forms of music associated with public festivals and performances.
- Some scholars and teachers felt that music heard solely

for the sheer delight of it was too much like secular music.
- Only vocal music was widely accepted in the church, originating with the chant although even vocal music was restricted in some churches.
- From the Middle Ages up to the 16th Century, the organ and some orchestral instruments continued to be used sparingly in various churches but there remained resistance to certain types of vocal and instrumental music and instrumental music was often banned from the churches.
- In the 16th Century in Italy, the Council of Trent passed measures aimed at purging the church. Musicians were accused of using inappropriate instruments in the services.
- During the German Reformation, Martin Luther wrote the 95 Theses in 1517. It is said to have called the organ a "sign of Baal." However, some churches continued to use the organ and other stringed instruments.
- It became customary in the 17th century to have parts played on the organ while the congregation sang. More important was the establishment of the oratorio and the development of instrumental church music, particularly the church sonata, which spread to England, Germany and France.
- In the period after 1750, the production of great church music became even scarcer. The oratorio, which found one of its greatest masters in Handel, is perhaps the only type of religious music that can boast an almost uninterrupted line of composers.
- It was during the performance of the "Hallelujah Chorus" from Handel's *Messiah* at Westminster Abbey in 1791 that Joseph Haydn was so deeply moved he burst into tears and exclaimed, "He is master of us all!" Haydn's appreciation for Handel is apparent in his works, particularly his oratorio *The Creation*.

For 2,000 years the church has struggled to try and figure out what is appropriate and what is inappropriate in this whole realm of worship, instruments and music. It helps us to understand that this problem is not new. I do not think there is anything that Satan hates more than when the church worships God. And I think Satan has found worship in the local church an area that he can exploit to his own advantage. Satan has found an area in our churches, an area that we take very personally, that he can use to create division.

There were occasions in Old Testament times when musical instruments were used by God's people for various purposes including worship. But there are no rules laid down as to the type of instruments that should be used or the type of music that should be played for worship. For example, the Psalmist simply states that it is possible for instruments to communicate in such a way that we worship. However, I must say to those who consider and argue that only quiet, solemn music is acceptable for worship that the Psalmist's reference to trumpets, tambourines and resonating and loud cymbals rather destroys your argument. And what about "tambourines and dancing" mentioned in verse 4? I do not think that the Psalmist had a nice quiet waltz in mind, do you? And if you know anything about Eastern dance and the type of dancing we read about in the days when the Psalms were written, you will realise that it would require and be accompanied by some very lively music.

Our dogs do not paint and do not appreciate paintings. They are not made in the image of God. But we are. The same thing is true of music.

Music does not have to have words in order to lead us in worship. Verse 6 says it well:

"Let everything that has breath praise the LORD. Praise the LORD!" Psalm 150:6.

Having written this, let me ask a question. We come together as the people of God and we worship Christ who is worthy to receive our worship. How many of us could honestly say that we go with our hearts and minds prepared? Do we really have in our hearts and minds the thought that *I am about to focus on Christ*?

It is very easy to get lost in the scramble of the day and just go through the motions and maybe, halfway through the service think, *Oh, maybe I should think about what I am doing here.* For worship to be meaningful, we have a responsibility to prepare our hearts and our minds. Only *we* can do that as those who have been redeemed enter into worship together.

May God have blessed you as you read this book.

Scripture taken from the

HOLY BIBLE
NEW INTERNATIONAL VERSIONS
Copyright 1973, 1978, 1984
International Bible Society.
Used by permission of Zondervan.
All rights reserved.

No part of this publication may be reproduced, stored in a retrieval system, or transmitted in any form or by any means, electronic, mechanical, photocopying, recording or otherwise without the prior permission of the copyright owner.

Good News Broadcasting Association (UK)
Ranskill DN22 8NN England
Email: info@gnba.net Web site: www.gnba.net

All rights reserved
Copyright Good News Broadcasting Association (UK)